The

Other Kind of Smart

The Other Kind of Smart

SIMPLE WAYS TO BOOST YOUR
EMOTIONAL INTELLIGENCE
FOR GREATER PERSONAL
EFFECTIVENESS AND SUCCESS

HARVEY DEUTSCHENDORF

AMACOM

American Management Association
New York • Atlanta • Brussels • Chicago • Mexico City • San Francisco
Shanghai • Tokyo • Toronto • Washington, D.C.

Special discounts on bulk quantities of AMACOM books are available to corporations, professional associations, and other organizations. For details, contact Special Sales Department, AMACOM, a division of American Management Association, 1601 Broadway, New York, NY 10019.
Tel: 212-903-8316. Fax: 212-903-8083.
E-mail: specialsls@amanet.org
Website: www.amacombooks.org/go/specialsales
To view all AMACOM titles go to: www.amacombooks.org

This publication is designed to provide accurate and authoritative information in regard to the subject matter covered. It is sold with the understanding that the publisher is not engaged in rendering legal, accounting, or other professional service. If legal advice or other expert assistance is required, the services of a competent professional person should be sought.

Library of Congress Cataloging-in-Publication Data

Deutschendorf, Harvey.
  The other kind of smart : simple ways to boost your emotional intelligence for greater personal effectiveness and success / Harvey Deutschendorf.
     p. cm.
  Includes bibliographical references and index.
  ISBN-13: 978-0-8144-1405-7 (pbk.)
  ISBN-10: 0-8144-1405-2 (pbk.)
  1. Emotional intelligence. 2. Success. I. Title.
  BF576.D48 2009
  152.4--dc22
                                        2009004045

Printing number

10 9 8 7 6 5 4 3 2 1

Contents

Acknowledgments

I would like to thank all of the people who have shared their stories for this book. It is through these stories that we have been able to bring emotional intelligence to life in the real world. Thanks to the Mankind Project for the inspiring and invaluable work that you carry out. It is truly life transforming.

Thanks to my agent, John Willig for believing in me and for his relentless efforts to place my work with the right publishing house. I appreciated the warm welcome that I received from Jacqueline Flynn, executive editor at AMACOM books. It was a pleasure working with Jennifer Holder, my editor. Her discerning eye, knowledge, and sense of teamwork greatly enhanced the strength of the original manuscript.

Thanks to all the pioneers who have discovered, developed, and refined the notion of emotional intelligence. I am grateful to Dr. Reuven BarOn for his groundbreaking work in developing the first scientific assessment tool for emotional intelligence, upon which this book is based. Also, thanks to Daniel Goleman, whose best-selling books on emotional intelligence created a great deal of public awareness and interest in the topic. All of your hard work is helping to make the world a better place to live.

Introduction

The most powerful tool is the one that people will use. The techniques in this book are simple, easy to understand and use, and will not demand a great deal of your time. I understand and respect the fact that you have a life with many diverse interests and limited time. Although you may have a strong interest in emotional intelligence, it must fit into your world, not the other way around. This book offers simple, effective techniques that will take five minutes per day.

Success is not a quantum leap. It is the accumulation of small changes resulting from perseverance, self-discipline, and learning to get the most from your emotional intelligence. When asked if it is difficult to increase one's emotional intelligence, the answer is yes and no. No, it is not technically difficult. It does not require special knowledge, a high IQ, or a lot of technical know-how. Yet it is not easy to do. It requires the self-discipline necessary to continually keep working over an extended period of time, even if the results are not immediately apparent. We may have been subconsciously working under self-destructive default modes for most of our lives. Many of our behavior modes were born out of necessity and survival mode to get us through difficult situations in our past. Many of us rely on anger and other strong emotions to cope with and escape dysfunctional families and other unfortunate situations that we are brought up with. Once we are out of the original family situation, however, the anger no longer serves us well and works against us. At that point, it is crucial that we recognize that thoughts and behaviors that were once necessary are now obsolete and harmful to us. We must then make an effort to develop new ways of thinking about ourselves, others, and our environment. What we pick up through our formative years while growing up impacts us for the rest of our lives—in our workplaces, in our homes, and in all of our interactions in the world.

Although some of what we have learned is positive and will serve us well, some may be sabotaging our future and limiting our potential for a successful and fulfilling life. The exciting news is that we can change what we have learned in the past and learn new and better ways of interacting with the world around us. Unlike the intelligence quotient (IQ), which is pretty much set for life by the time we reach adulthood, we can change our emotional intelligence (EI).

The first step is identifying what our strengths are and what serves us well. In his book *Go Put Your Strengths to Work*, author Marcus Buckingham tells us that we should focus on creating a work environment that uses more of our strengths and spends less time on our weaknesses.

His theory suggests that it is much more beneficial to us to focus upon, and improve on, areas that we are naturally good at and have a talent for. This viewpoint goes along with the positive psychology movement, which tells us that we will achieve much better results in helping others if we concentrate on their strengths rather than on their weaknesses. This is a significant change from the past in which psychology focused mainly on weaknesses and how to improve on them. Overall, I think that focusing on our strengths is the way to go. Whenever I am giving feedback on an EI assessment with someone or coaching, I first identify and speak to that person's strengths before looking at areas that are challenges. While focusing on strengths, however, there are certain areas that we cannot afford to ignore even if we find we are not strong in them. These critical areas will sabotage us and negate our strengths if we don't manage them well.

The question of why some people become successful, while others struggle throughout their lives and achieve little has always fascinated mankind. During most of the twentieth century we were led to believe that it was our cognitive intelligence, or IQ, that determined how well we would do in life. Yet, our common sense and simple power of observation tells us that this simply cannot be the case—that there must be more to success than how well we do in exams at school.

In *Successful Intelligence*, Robert Sternberg looks at the case of two Yale graduates and how they fared in the real world. Penn was brilliant in his classes and creative, being able to come up with ideas of his own. He was, strictly in academic terms, the best to come out of Yale. There was only one problem, Penn was quite arrogant and almost completely lacking in practical skills.

Even though Penn was interviewed by all of the top companies, his arrogance assured that he wasn't called back with job offers. His only offer came from a second-rate company where he lasted for only three years.

On the other hand, Penn's roommate Matt was not as strong academically but had a great deal of social intelligence. Matt received seven offers from eight interviews. Although not brilliant, he has been a reliable performer and his social skills have allowed his career to flourish.

Think back to your high school days. Remember the bright kids who had great marks and everyone expected them to do great things in the world? Did they do as well as everyone expected? What about the kids whom everyone laughed at because they dropped out of school to sell used cars? Did you find in going back to a reunion that the bright kid is driving a taxicab while the dropout is a multimillionaire?

We all know versions of this story. All of us know people who were very bright, according to their grades in school, but have struggled to fit into society. The Unabomber, Ted Kaczynski, and the other infamous Ted, Ted Bundy, are just two of the many well-known examples of this outcome. On the other hand, we probably know someone who would likely not score all that high on an IQ test but is doing quite well. The notion, therefore, that there are other factors that come into play, besides IQ, in determining a person's success should not come as a surprise to most of us. We have watched this happen all of our lives.

For example, in *Working with Emotional Intelligence*, Daniel Goleman looks at the files of a consulting company to find the devastating results of a lack of impulse control. These case studies of wrecked careers come from the files of a consulting company that assessed each of these executives in the course of testing 4,265 people, from company heads to blue-collar workers.

Among the findings from Goleman's list is the case of a corporate controller who was quite aggressive with everyone with whom he came into contact. He was eventually fired because of a complaint of sexual harassment from a female employee who reported to him. In another case, an exceptionally extroverted executive, known for his outgoing, gregarious manner, pushed the boundaries of confidentiality and ended up being fired for publicly releasing confidential company information. There is also the matter of a CEO and his hand-picked CFO who were both fired due to mismanagement of company funds. Both were lacking in ethics and had little concern about the effects of their actions.

All of these people had a lack of impulse control, with little or no ability to delay gratification. With self-restraint, people can think through potential consequences of what they are about to do and assume responsibility for their words and deeds.

The consulting firm that did the study of self-restraint in professions recommends that "when selecting people for industrial jobs—at all levels—it is wise to reject candidates who are low or very low" in self-restraint, since "the odds of them creating problems of some kind are extremely high." (The firm does note, though, that people can be helped to handle their impulsivity better—poor impulse control need not be a sentence to a dead-end career.)[1]

Many an otherwise successful career, marriage, relationship, and friendship have been ruined by someone, in a moment of anger, speaking words on the spur of the moment that they spend a lifetime regretting. It is therefore crucial to identify areas that have the potential to sabotage us and at the very least neutralize them so that they do not become roadblocks on the road to our success.

Unfortunately, our minds are not programmed like computers; we cannot simply log in and change the settings within seconds. We can develop new defaults, however, by constantly practicing better ways of dealing with issues. Over time, these techniques will become easier and feel more like a part of who we are. As our new techniques become more natural and a part of us, the former thoughts and behaviors will start to seem unnatural and unfamiliar.

At this point we will know that an authentic, lasting change is taking shape within our lives and changing us for the better. Eventually these new patterns will become our new default, coming to us automatically and naturally.

Note

1. Daniel Goleman, *Working with Emotional Intelligence* (New York: Bantam Books, 1998), p. 92.

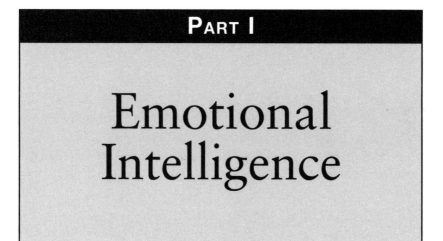

PART I

Emotional Intelligence

CHAPTER 1

What Is EI?

"The greatest discovery of my generation is that
human beings can alter their lives by changing
the attitude of the mind."

—WILLIAM JAMES, PSYCHOLOGIST AND PHILOSOPHER

The idea that our emotions influence how well we do in life is not new. It has been around as long as humans have been on earth. The ancient Greek philosophers spoke of the impact that emotions had on themselves and on those around them. In the last few decades, we have made major breakthroughs in the study of our emotions and their effect on our lives.

History of a Concept

During the early part of the twentieth century, researchers and psychologists seriously began to study various forms of general intelligence. By the time the IQ test was established and being used in schools, David Wechsler, who developed the latest version of the IQ test in 1940, already felt that there were other areas of intelligence that needed to be measured. He inferred that one of the areas we needed to look at was what is now called *emotional intelligence*. In 1955, Albert Ellis, the founder of rational-emotive therapy, speculated that people could learn to deal with their emotions by using their rationale. In 1980, Dr. Reuven BarOn, an Israeli psychologist and Rhodes Scholar, began to study how emotions affect people's functioning.

Using his own work and that of earlier researchers, BarOn began to develop the emotional quotient, or EQ test, for emotional intelligence, the first scientifically valid assessment for emotional intelligence. The American Psychological Association approved the test, known as the BarOn EQ-i®, or Emotional Quotient Inventory.

The term *emotional intelligence* is credited to John Mayer of the University of New Hampshire and Peter Salovey of Yale University. In 1990, the two psychology professors, along with colleague David Caruso, developed an alternate test for emotional intelligence. Their test, the Mayer-Salovey-Caruso Emotional Intelligence Test (MSCEIT), is an ability-based test of emotional intelligence. The discussion around who actually discovered emotional intelligence or who first coined the term is a moot point. Our knowledge base had progressed to the point that researchers and social scientists were making new breakthroughs in the area of human functioning. With our new understanding, it was becoming possible to measure and test for the effects of emotions in our lives in an accurate and meaningful way.

Think of it as being similar to technical breakthroughs such as the automobile or airplane. Although the Wright brothers have gone down in history as the first to achieve sustained airborne flight, there were others who were working on this and close to achieving flight. Technology had advanced to the point that airborne flight was possible and there were inventors at that time in all the industrial nations such as England, France, and Germany who were getting close to achieving a breakthrough. If the Wright brothers had not made their historic flight in Kitty Hawk, it is likely that someone would have flown shortly after that time. It was an idea whose time had come. The same principle applies to emotional intelligence.

In 1995 Daniel Goleman published *Emotional Intelligence*, which summed up the work that had been done up to that point in the field. It became a bestseller, and Goleman appeared as a guest on the *Oprah Winfrey Show*. If there was a defining moment for emotional intelligence, this was it. Public awareness of the concept, which up until this point had been minuscule, jumped dramatically. People began to talk about emotional intelligence as articles began to appear in major magazines such as *Time* and *Newsweek*.

In 1998, Goleman followed up his highly successful first book with *Emotional Intelligence in the Workplace*, in which he researched how businesses were benefiting from implementing emotional intelligence concepts in the workplace. Like his first book, this one also became successful and the author again appeared on *Oprah*. In the last few years, articles have appeared in prestigious business publications such as the *Harvard Business Review* and *Fast Company*, quickly clearing up any misconceptions that emotional intelligence is some "fuzzy, feel good" idea that has no place in the real world.

Misconceptions

Since the term *emotional intelligence* has been around, there have been some misconceptions regarding what it means. Without digging further and investigating as to what the term actually means, people have jumped to conclusions based solely on their connotations of the word *emotional*. In the book *Working with Emotional Intelligence*, Daniel Goleman attempts to set the record straight and clear up some misconceptions surrounding the term emotional intelligence.

Playing Nice

Rather than simply being nice, emotional intelligence means being real, open, and honest regarding our feelings. This can take courage as it is often easier to skirt around issues than to confront them directly. Rather, we need to be real in our interactions with others. While we should be sensitive to other people's feelings, ignoring or overlooking their negative or destructive behavior does them no favors. If we truly care about someone, we must be forthright and honest even though it may be uncomfortable for us at the time and not appreciated. True friends will end up appreciating that we had the courage, and cared enough, to be honest with them.

Letting It All Hang Out

As Goleman points out, "Emotional intelligence does not mean giving free rein to feelings—*'letting it all hang out.'* Rather, it means managing feelings so that they are expressed appropriately and effectively, enabling people to work together smoothly toward common goals."[1]

There is a time and place for expressing strong emotional feelings to others. For example, during a staff meeting is not the right time or place to vent anger at a coworker. Later, once we are calmed down and have carefully thought out what we are going to say and are in a private setting with the coworker would be a much better time and place.

Women Have More Emotional Intelligence

Another aspect of EI that is frequently misunderstood is the differences between the genders' natural ability to express it. Women in our society have always had a great deal more freedom and permission to express and show their emotions than men. This is slowly starting to change as Western culture has been waking up to the negative consequences of not allowing men to openly express their emotions. Because women have been much more open and expressive in general with their emotions, it is assumed by some that they will be better in all areas of EI than men. Daniel Goleman tried to clear up misconceptions regarding gender differences when he wrote that "women are not 'smarter' than men when it comes to emotional intelligence, nor are men superior to women. Each of us has a personal profile of strengths and weaknesses in these capacities. Some of us may be highly empathic but lack some abilities to handle our own distress; others may be quite aware of the subtlest shift in our own moods, yet be inept socially."[2]

When we add up male/female profiles, we find that women on the whole are more aware of their emotions and are better at forming relationships with others while men adapt more easily and handle stress better. However, it is important to remember that this finding does not account for individual variations where these differences could be reversed. There are men who are very aware of their emotions and are able to form strong relationships, just as there are women who adapt easily and are good at handling stress.

Emotional Intelligence Is Not Fixed at Birth

The most exciting and promising aspect of emotional intelligence is that we are able to change it. In other words, unlike our IQ, we are not stuck with what we are born with. The great news about EQ is that it is not fixed or only developed at a certain stage in life. It has been shown that life experiences can be used to increase EQ and that we can continue to develop our capacity to learn and adapt as we grow older. The EQ realm is one area that does reward us for successfully having gone through stages of our lives.

Note

1. Daniel Goleman, *Working with Emotional Intelligence* (New York: Bantam Books, 1998), p. 6.
2. Ibid, p. 7.

CHAPTER 2

The Business Connection

"If you are working for a company that is not enthusiastic, energetic, creative, clever, curious, and just plain fun, you've got troubles, serious troubles."

—TOM PETERS, MANAGEMENT GURU

Up until now, the emotional intelligence movement has been largely driven by business and industry, where leaders have been quick to recognize the benefits of higher emotional intelligence levels in their managers and employees. Simply put, there is a direct connection between an employee's level of EI and his or her productivity. Being able to effectively work with others in an organization is one of the most sought-after skills in any organization. When employers are asked to name the top skills they look for in employees, people skills always rank at the top. Although technical skills can be taught, it is much more difficult to change someone's attitude or people-relationship skills.

The challenges facing business today are huge. Studies and statistics show that many companies are a far cry from the ideal type of workplace described by management guru Tom Peters. According to an article in *Psychology Today*, up to 40 percent of employee turnover is related to stress and up to a million workers per day are off due to problems that can be linked to stress. The estimated cost of this loss of productivity to the U.S. economy is estimated to be close to $200 billion. The Yale School of Management completed a survey that found 24 percent of the working population reported that they were chronically angry at work. With these kinds of realities facing the workplace today, it is little wonder that companies are desperately looking for ways to create healthier, better functioning work environments.

From an employer perspective, the results are no more promising. In *Working with Emotional Intelligence*, Daniel Goleman reveals the results of a survey of U.S. employers that showed they struggle to find the right type of employees. Forty percent of employees had trouble working with colleagues and less than 20 percent had the work habit and discipline needed for entry-level jobs. Employers increasingly complain about the lack of people skills in the people they hire. Giving younger employees feedback at evaluation time has been a problem, as many seem to view constructive criticism as an attack on them personally and become angry. This problem is not confined to new employees and youth. To become successful in the 1960s and 1970s, it was required that one attend the right schools and obtain good marks. As a result many executives have risen to high positions without having developed good emotional intelligence and find their careers have peaked or even deconstructed.

Emotions in the Workplace

As early as 1935, Australian psychologist Edgar Doll expounded on his theory that emotions motivated and drove us to achieve. They were therefore an important part of our working lives as well as our lives outside of work. Our understanding of emotions at the time was not advanced enough for the world to be ready to hear his pronouncements. It would take decades before Doll's ideas became widely accepted.

Not that many years ago, it was expected that our emotions had no place in the workplace and that we checked them at the door once we arrived at work. One of the reasons given for excluding women from the workforce was that they were too emotional, which would prevent them from functioning effectively in the workplace. Although that view seems antiquated today, it was only today's baby boom generation of females who became integrated into the workforce in a major way. The idea that our emotions have no place in the workplace sounds about as obsolete as the idea that smoking has no relationship to cancer. However, many workplaces are uncomfortable with the idea that our emotions are part of who we are and affect everything we do. They seem to still operate under the notion that it is possible to keep emotions outside of work. Success in business basically comes down to our ability to form effective relationships with others. These others include our colleagues, managers, employees, and customers. The companies that are able to form the best relationships, both internally among their employees and externally with customers and suppliers, are the most successful.

I am not sure if Herb Kelleher and the founders of Southwest Airlines had ever heard of Edgar Doll when they struggled against all odds to start a fledgling airline in Texas in 1971. What they knew, however, was what it took to motivate people in the workplace. From the beginning, their belief was that your people give as good as they get. If you genuinely care for your employees, put them before anything else, they will repay you with amazing loyalty and effort. The end result is a highly successful organization.

Case Study: Southwest Airlines

An example of a company that has done an excellent job of tapping into emotional intelligence to create a dynamic, fun-loving, family-oriented work environment is Southwest Airlines. This organization has been widely studied as an example of how to create a healthy work culture. The reason that Southwest Airlines receives the attention it does is because not only is it a great place to work but it is also a highly successful organization that just so happens to be a socially responsible employer that genuinely cares for its employees.

The success of the airline, however, is what garners so much attention from business circles. Founded in 1971 as a short haul carrier based out of Love Field in Dallas, its financial success story has been truly remarkable. Since 1973, it has shown a profit every year while most other airlines were unable to string together more than a couple of years of profit in a very turbulent, changeable industry. Even after the September 11, 2001 terrorist attacks, when other airlines suffered, Southwest expanded its market share. While other airlines laid off thousands of staff, Southwest, as it has consistently managed to do, kept its entire staff. This was in keeping with the airline's tradition of looking after its people.

The business press has noticed and frequently commented on the success of Southwest. *Fortune* magazine called it "the most successful airline in history."[1]

Although this maverick airline has been able to achieve its success through many innovative and create methods, it is the people aspect of the company that will be focused on in this book. Southwest has consistently had lower turnover rates than other competitors and has consistently scored higher on employee satisfaction surveys. For three years in a row, it has been included in *Fortune* magazine's list of the "100 Best Companies to Work For in America." Many companies have attempted to emulate Southwest's business practices. Ultimately, however, the people who work for an organization are what make it work. The success of any organization depends on the relationships it develops among management, staff, customers, and suppliers. Emulating business practices is a relatively easy task compared with building a culture that creates a family of loyal, dedicated, hardworking employees who genuinely care for their jobs, each other, and the customers whom they serve.

After the massive layoffs that took place with other airlines after September 11, 2001, one longtime Southwest airline employee remarked that it was not surprising that his airline did not let anyone go. He told the reporter interviewing him that it was part of the culture that they did whatever they had to do to look after their people. Such a culture does not come about by accident, but by consistently applying principles and actions over time that show staff they are cared about and allows them to use and develop their potential.

All aspects of our lives are interrelated. What happens at home affects how we perform at work and what happens at work affects our home lives. Yet, many workplaces continue to operate as if it is possible to separate our work lives from everything else that is going on in our world.

Southwest Airlines recognizes the interconnectedness of all areas of life and makes an effort to bring the families of their employees into their workplace. Family picnics and events are held regularly and birthdays, weddings, and births are celebrated. Whenever possible, family members are invited to learn more about the workplace and what the employees do there. While other companies pay lip service to their staff being part of a family, Southwest Airlines has a committee, called the Culture Committee, whose role is to come up with ways to make employees and their families feel like they are part of the organization. It is also recognized that there is also a danger of an employee spending so much time focused on work that his or her family will suffer. Employees can use work as a means of refuge from an unhappy family situation. Companies such as Southwest Airlines that recognize the importance of a work-life balance end up with happier, more productive employees.

The Secret to Great Leadership

"Trust men and they will be true to you; treat them greatly and they will show themselves great."

—Ralph Waldo Emerson,
American Essayist, Philosopher, and Poet

Robin Sharma, after presenting to business audiences, is often asked about a statement that he makes indicating that we are all leaders. He replies that one thing that separates the best companies from the rest is the rate at which high-performing companies develop leaders. They develop them faster than everyone else.[2] Although not everyone will lead the entire organization, every single employee is a leader in his or her own sphere of influence.

In these companies, every person on the staff is empowered to act like a leader. They are encouraged to take ownership of their areas of responsibility and raise their performance up to a level of excellence. They see to it that employees are committed to superb service and see change as an opportunity to do things better.

Charles Schwab has the distinction of being one of the first CEOs in business to earn over a million dollars a year as the first president of United States Steel. Although this amount may seem puny by today's standards, this was back in 1921 when fifty dollars a week was considered to be a good salary.

In his timeless bestseller *How to Win Friends & Influence People,* Dale Carnegie interviewed Schwab. According to Schwab:

> I consider my ability to arouse enthusiasm among my people the greatest asset I possess, and the way to develop the best that is in a person is by appreciation and encouragement.
>
> There is nothing else that kills the ambitions of a person as much as criticism from superiors. I never criticize anyone. I believe in giving a person incentive to work. So I am anxious to praise but loath to find fault. If I like anything, *I am hearty in my approbation and lavish in my praise.*[3]

That is what Schwab did. But what do average people do? The exact opposite. If they don't like something, they bawl out their subordinates, but if they do like it, they say nothing. As the old couplet says: "Once I did bad that I hear ever/Twice I did good, but that I hear never."[4]

I admit, when I first read about Southwest Airlines, I became teary eyed. I believe deep down that we all want to be able to give our all and have dreams of finding an organization that deserves everything that we have to give. In other words, it's finding an organization that we willingly give everything for because they will give everything for us.

Whether at work or at home, we all have a need to be loved and cared about. It is a basic human need. Southwest recognizes that our work effects our home and vice versa. We cannot separate people into segments; we have a responsibility to look after the whole person. In *Lessons in Loyalty*, former Southwest executive Lorraine Grubbs-West explains her organization's philosophy:

> At Southwest Airlines, employees are accepted and treated as "whole people." Its leaders realize their employees' personal lives cannot be separated from their work lives, nor do they want that to happen. Personal challenges affect people, and Southwest's leaders realize it is unreasonable to expect people to stifle life's difficult circumstances for the sake of their jobs.[5]

Recruiting

One of the chief areas where companies have used emotional intelligence is in recruiting new employees. Human resources departments have incorporated EI concepts into their interviewing questions, and some have used versions of tests developed to assess EI. Recruiting, interviewing, and choosing the right people have always been challenges for organizations. Despite tools developed to help human resources people make better decisions, the selection process is still hit or miss at the best of times. As human resources people develop better and more effective methods of screening for and interviewing applicants, job seekers are becoming more sophisticated in their approach to interviews. The more evolved interviewing processes become, the more adept interviewees become at giving the answers that human resources people are looking for. In other words, there will always be people who will be able to "snow" the people interviewing them. As interviewing processes become more advanced, so will the ability of the people who will always be looking for ways to "beat" the system. Another factor that is making selection more difficult is the increasing frustration that human resources people are feeling in getting adequate reference checks. After a number of highly publicized cases of former employees successfully suing their former employers for giving them bad references, human resources people have become very cautious about what information they give out.

Often the information is so limited that it is of little use to the person asking the questions. Afraid of lawsuits, organizations are becoming very shy about giving out information about former employees that would put them in a negative light. Yet, this is exactly the type of information that human resources people need to make the right decisions.

Although many organizations claim that they hire for attitude and train for skills, Southwest Airlines really does. How they are able to do this is not well understood or widely practiced. When Southwest opened a new operation in Raleigh, North Carolina, the company approached a local recruiting agency and told them Southwest was hiring for attitude and training for skills. At first, this philosophy stumped the agency, which continued to ask what skills the airline was looking for. Southwest decided that the best way to get the idea across to the recruiters was to have them spend some time with Southwest employees. After doing so, the recruiters had a clear picture of what kind of people Southwest was searching for. Southwest believes that actions speak louder than words. As a result, many unsuitable candidates are screened out before they go for the formal interview. Before the interview, potential employees visit different areas of the organization and talk to staff involved in various functions. Unbeknownst to the job seeker, this is actually part of the interview. They are being observed to see how well they interact with others and to determine how well they fit into the Southwest culture. Any sign of rudeness or arrogance to any employee is noted and becomes a disqualifier, regardless of the qualifications that the person may have to do the job.

A story went around about a highly qualified military pilot who had applied for work and was being shown around the work site. During his rounds he was rude to an administrative person and displayed arrogance to one of the maintenance people. As a result, he was not hired despite his impressive technical qualifications.

Southwest puts very high value on interpersonal relationships—that is, the ability of people to get along with one another. In many cases, applicants will disqualify themselves, realizing that they do not fit into the culture. Invariably, hiring mistakes do happen, even with the best screening and intentions. In many cases, individuals themselves feel out of place in the Southwest environment and look for work elsewhere. In other cases, human resources acts quickly and removes the person, allowing him or her as much dignity and self-respect as possible. Southwest's consist record of lower turnover and higher employee satisfaction ratings compared with other airlines is a good indicator that they are getting their hiring practices right a great deal of the time.

Humans are incredibly complicated, making the job of human resources vastly challenging. The value of coming up with a better way to assess how someone will perform in a job is huge. The cost of hiring the wrong people is so debilitating to organizations that any development that promises to increase the odds of hiring better staff was bound to receive intense interest.

The Soft Stuff Is Important

Six Seconds, an international not-for-profit organization, completed a report on workplace issues in 1997. Researchers interviewed 135 organizations ranging in size from 20 to 10,000. Leaders, from executives to team leaders, were asked to identify the major challenges that workplaces today face.

They found that the "soft" people-related issues, such as finding and keeping talent, were three times more serious than issues unrelated to people, such as finance.

The results indicated that emotional intelligence and feelings both within and outside the organization were among the most important strengths an organization had for overcoming challenges and reaching their goals. Recruiting and keeping good people, as well as letting go of people who were a bad fit, were seen as a top priority for three-quarters of those interviewed. The same number indicated that creating a positive work culture was very important. The vast majority of the leaders interviewed said that team members' feelings were either essential or highly important when it came to dealing with issues that the organization faced. When the researchers asked about the feelings and attitudes of people outside of the organization, they received similar results. An overwhelming majority of those surveyed said they felt that EQ was essential or highly important in dealing with the main challenges that the organization faced. None of the respondents indicated that it was "not important" and only a small number rated it as "less than highly important."

Companies and corporations have not simply jumped on the EI bandwagon because it sounded good or was the flavor of the month in human resources development circles. There is solid and compelling research showing a strong relationship between performance levels and EI competencies. This relationship, of course, directly affects the bottom line. A number of studies have shown a strong relationship between EI and performance levels at the workplace and job success. All of the following studies can be found online at the website of the Consortium for Research on Emotional Intelligence (www.eiconsortium.org).

In one study of more than three hundred top-level executives from fifteen global companies, research showed that strong emotional competencies distinguished star performers from average ones. It was discovered in jobs considered to be of medium complexity, such as sales clerks and mechanics, that top performers were twelve times more productive than those at the bottom and 85 percent more productive than the average performer. In the most complex jobs, such as insurance salespeople and account managers, top performers were 127 percent more productive than an average performer. Research in more than two hundred companies and corporations worldwide suggested that about one-third of the differences were due to technical skills and cognitive ability while the remaining two-thirds were due to emotional competence.[6] In top leadership positions, it was found that over four-fifths of the difference was due to emotional competence. When L'Oréal began selecting salespeople on the basis of certain emotional competencies, they did a cross comparison of the staff they hired using this method versus those hired using the old standard selection procedure. It was found that those selected using emotional competence sold on average over $91,000 annually more than those hired by using traditional methods. It was also found that they had 63 percent less turnover than the group hired using the former method. A national insurance company compared the performance of sales agents with different levels of emotional competencies. Those who were very strong in at least five of eight areas of key emotional competencies sold

$114,000 worth of insurance versus $54,000 worth sold by those weak in those competencies.[7]

Team-building and staff development programs have also benefited. Just a few of the major corporations that have used EI are IBM, American Express, and AT&T.

In 2000 Daniel Goleman co-authored another EI book, called *Primal Leadership*. EI has become firmly established in many corporate and government leadership programs. You would be hard pressed today to find a major leadership program in North America that does not incorporate EI principles.

Notes

1. Katrina Brooker, "The Chairman of the Board Looks Back," *Fortune Magazine* (May 28, 2001).
2. Robin Sharma, *Greatness Guide Book 2* (New York: HarperCollins, 2007), p. 38.
3. Dale Carnegie, *How to Win Friends & Influence People* (New York: Simon & Schuster, 1971), p. 24.
4. Ibid.
5. Lorraine Grubbs-West, *Lessons in Loyalty: How Southwest Airlines Does It—An Insider's View* (Dallas: CornerStone Leadership Institute, 2005), p. 84.
6. Consortium for Research on Emotional Intelligence, www.eiconsortium.org.
7. Hay/McBer Research and Innovation Group, 1997.

CHAPTER 3

Inspiring Workplaces

"You can handle people more successfully by enlisting their
feelings than by convincing their reason."

—AUTHOR PAUL P. PARKER

I magine a workplace where everyone wanted to come to work and where the time flew by because everyone was enthusiastic and worked together to do challenging and exciting things. For most employees this sounds like a fairy tale, something that is not possible to achieve in the real world. Yet, there are workplaces that strive to reach the type of workplace where humanity and concern for employees and customers is the actual walk instead of just talk. Open and progressive companies encourage their staff to openly express emotions and provide a safe environment for them to do so. The old way of thinking that workplaces should be cold and logical places where emotions have no place has resulted in highly dysfunctional, tense, and unhealthy workplaces. People are naturally emotional and need the opportunity to release these emotions in a safe and timely manner. Allowing employees to express their frustrations, anger, and disappointments can lead to better relationship building and more energy and effort being focused on finding solutions. However, it is crucial that employees feel safe. Any repercussions, or hints or rumors of repercussions, will quickly shut down the lines of open and honest sharing of emotions. If they are unable to express negative emotions, employees keep these emotions inside where they fester, grow, and turn into a destructive force.

A workplace with a lot of buried strong emotions is a dangerous place just waiting to erupt. When employees are not allowed to express their emotions, they often build up and are acted upon. Instead of concentrating on their work, employees are looking for opportunities to get back at their organization, their boss, or their fellow employees.

Not only is this type of workplace bad for morale and the psychological well-being of those who work there, it is an unproductive organization. The extreme examples of repressed emotions being acted out are the cases where an employee goes on a killing rampage at the work site. Although it can be argued that these individuals have psychological issues, it points to the need to allow people the opportunity to vent and release their emotions in a safe environment.

Conflict in the Workplace

Although many workplaces view conflict as being negative, it is a sign that the employee is alive, engaged, and passionate. The alternative to engaging such an employee is to have the person totally disengaged from the workplace, being there in person but not in spirit. Workplace conflict, if handled properly, can lead to better relationships between conflicting parties. Often conflict can come from miscommunication and misunderstanding. It is important that the focus of resolving conflict be on resolving the issue and forming better relationships rather than assigning blame. If resolved effectively, conflict can result in better understanding and appreciation of other perspectives and result in stronger relationships in the workplace. Being able to resolve conflict can result in an increase of goodwill and understanding and strengthen the bonds in a relationship.

Robin Sharma speaks about our attempts to avoid conflict at all costs. The problem with conflict, he says, is that it never repairs itself; it never just goes away on its own. Rather than viewing conflict as a negative thing to stay away from, Sharma sees it as a way to get closer to others. Because we are interacting with others on a more intense and deep level there is an opportunity to connect in ways that normal, everyday interactions just do not allow for. Out of conflict can grow increased self-awareness and personal growth. While it takes courage to face conflict head-on when our impulse is to avoid it, the rewards of working through it are immense.[1]

Regardless of the types of people who are put together in a workplace, there will always be conflict. At Southwest, conflict is dealt with quickly and the two parties are brought together by a mediator. Each person listens to the other's point of view. More often than not, the conflict was a result of a misunderstanding, what was heard by one person was different from what the speaker intended to say. It is understood that the purpose of the mediation is to find solutions and to develop better working relationships, not to assign blame or find fault. It is important that everyone leaves the meeting with their self-worth intact.

Instead of being divisive and tearing an organization apart, conflict, if handled properly, can bring people closer together. It is not uncommon for two people who are conflicted to form a closer relationship after the conflict. Having gone through intense emotions together, they feel a stronger connection with and appreciation for one another. Conflict means that people are actively engaged and involved. It's when staff members disengage and stop caring that organizations need to be very concerned.

While attending college, I earned a little extra money driving a limousine part-time. The company I worked for had a contract for a restaurant chain that had several restaurants in the city. Wednesday night was ladies night, with drink specials and other special treats to try and entice female customers. Every ladies night included a draw for a free limousine ride with champagne and dinner for two at another restaurant location on the opposite side of the city. My company had the contract to provide the service. One evening as I got back from doing the restaurant transfer, my boss told me about a situation that occurred between him and the owner of the restaurant. The owner had called him, angrily complaining about the service that we were providing him. In all conversations with the restaurant owner prior to this there had been no indication that he was unhappy with the limousine company. On a number of occasions the owner had actually had positive things to say about my work and had received compliments from the customers that I had shuttled between the restaurants. My boss noticed that the owner wasn't able to articulate exactly what the problem was. My employer listened and did not get defensive or drawn in by the anger directed at him from the other end of the phone. Suspecting that he was angry about something other than our service, he calmly asked him who he was mad at. Then the real issue came out. The owner was upset with the fact that often people who won free draws did not show up and did not call to tell him that they were not coming. Since he had to pay for the limousine service regardless of whether or not the contest winners showed up, he was upset at what he considered to be the thoughtlessness and lack of gratitude of the no-shows. Since they were his customers, he was afraid to confront them, fearing that he would lose their business and the business of their friends whom they would almost certainly complain to. The younger female customers tended to come in groups, and the owner was concerned that if he upset one of them the whole group would stop coming to his establishment. Unable to take his frustrations out on his customers, he called my employer to vent. My boss could relate to his frustration, being in a situation himself where people often did not show up after promising to do so. After being able to release his frustration, he told my boss that he thought we were doing a great job and he was happy with the service. My boss's ability to tune in to what was going on emotionally with the manager resulted in his company continuing on with the contract and having a better working relationship with the restaurant owner.

The Importance of Emotional Connections

"Kind words can be short and easy to speak, but their echoes are truly endless."

—MOTHER TERESA

Managers at all levels can do a great deal to demonstrate that expressing emotions is acceptable by doing so themselves. In doing so, those under them will see their managers as being more open, real, and genuine, and

28

they will trust their managers more. Although they may not get their way, it is important that every employee get their say. A free flow of ideas is essential so that organizations are able to get maximum value from their staff. No idea should be dismissed as being too small, silly, or irrelevant. In this way, organizations can create an open and creative atmosphere.

Although the use of e-mail has become the primary form of communication in many work sites, face-to-face communication is the most effective way to build healthy relationships, both internally and with customers. In order to build trust and respect, we have to make an emotional connection with the person we are interacting with.

Note

1. Robin Sharma, *Greatness Guide Book 2* (New York: HarperCollins, 2007), p. 48.

CHAPTER 4

Success Throughout Your Life

"Caring is a powerful business advantage."

—Scott Johnson, Cartoonist, Illustrator, and Designer

Stewart D. Friedman, a Practice Professor of Management at the University of Pennsylvania's Wharton School in Philadelphia, directs Wharton's Leadership Program and Work/Life Integration Project. The aim of the program is to help people improve their performance in all domains of their lives including work, home, community, and self. This holistic approach recognizes the fact that we cannot separate one area of our lives from the other. If we excel at work at the expense of our home environment, eventually our home life will suffer and impact our work.

Traditional thinking has separated work and the other areas of our lives and often pitted one against the other. For better or worse, all areas of our lives are intertwined. The good news is that regardless of where we put our energies and efforts into increasing our EI functioning, whether at work, at home, or in the community, all areas of our life will improve. Throughout the book, you will find stories and examples of EI at the workplace, at home, and in the community. Sometimes the stories will connect all three areas to demonstrate how EI affects all areas of our lives. There is no such thing as trading off in one area, or giving it short shrift to benefit another area. By building better relationships in one area of our lives, it increases our capacity and ability to build in other areas, thereby leading to a more fulfilling life.

There is evidence that the more arenas of our lives in which we practice new behaviors, the more effective we will become in all areas of our lives. And the more areas of our lives that we can relate to leadership, the more quickly we will improve. According to Professor Jane Wheeler of the Weatherhead School of Management of Case Western Reserve University, the more venues in which people practiced new skills such as their families, community, and church, the greater was their improvement rate. Not only that, but these improvements seemed to stick around for a longer time, some still very much in evidence after a period of two years or more.

EI for the Twenty-First Century

Although the study of EI is still in its infancy, there is growing evidence that the study of emotions and how they affect our world will expand to many areas in the next few years.

Recently, the department for children, schools, and families in the United Kingdom implemented a SEAL program in their public school system. SEAL stands for Social, Emotional Aspects of Learning. Bullying has been a problem in the British school system as it has been in North America. It became apparent that the school system was not teaching one of the crucial skills that children need to learn to become well-adjusted adults, which is how to get along with others. The British school system set up a Social, Emotional, and Behavior Skills team to come up with programs that would effectively teach school-age children the social and emotional skills necessary to get along with their classmates and teachers. The hope was that once these skills were learned, the children would grow up to become well-adjusted functioning adults. School systems in other countries will be watching, and if the results are positive, will look at implementing similar type programs.

Interest in the value of EI has not been confined to the public school system. Institutions of higher education have been looking into ways that EI can be incorporated into the halls of advanced education. In 2008, Georgetown University in Washington, D.C., hosted a symposium with the objective of exploring the role of emotional intelligence in higher education. In this event the faculty, administrators, and students shared best practices, success stories, and ways that EI could be used to have a substantial impact on the success and development of students. Across the border in Canada, Wilfred Laurier University recently hosted a daylong event to discuss how EI impacted teaching and learning.

Ongoing research and study regarding EI is not confined to North America but is going on around the world. Recently, a study was conducted in a large urban hospital in Bologna, Italy, within the obstetrics department. The study showed a significant increase in performance and life success among professionals with high EI scores over those with lower scores. EI has also been finding its way into the highly competitive professional sports world. The Southampton Football Club in the English premier league has been using EI to develop their young talent. A study carried out at the National Chung Cheng University in Taiwan found a relationship among EI, physical activity, and health-related physical fitness. They found that students who had higher levels of EI were also more fit.

In short, emotional intelligence has become a highly valued commodity throughout the world in business, life, and leisure. The skills presented in this book can be applied throughout your life, whatever your profession, family situation, geography, or personality.

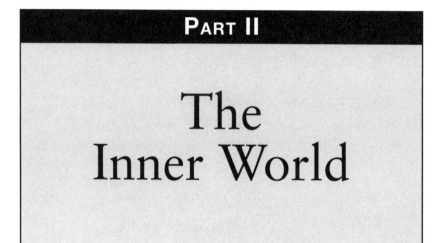

PART II

The Inner World

CHAPTER 5

Emotional Self-Awareness

"The first principle is that you must not fool yourself
and you are the easiest person to fool."

—Richard Feynman, American Physicist
and Nobel Laureate

"A satirist is a man who discovers unpleasant things about
himself and then says them about other people."

—Author Peter McArthur

Research has shown that greater emotional intelligence leads to increased fulfillment and success in life, and the journey begins within us. Unless we have first done this work on ourselves, we will be limited in our attempts to apply this work in the rest of our lives. Knowledge of our inner landscape helps us to realistically look at how we deal with others and the environment around us. A certain degree of understanding and the ability to manage our emotions is essential before we are able to effectively change other areas of our lives.

The amount of work we will have to do, and the effort necessary for us to change our inner landscape, depends on where we are starting from. Of course, the environment that we are raised in determines to a large part how we view ourselves and the world around us. People who have grown up in dysfunctional families will have developed coping mechanisms that do not serve them well in the larger world. They will require a longer period to come to terms with their emotions and learn to deal with them than someone who was raised in a relatively healthy environment.

Awareness of Our Emotions

Before we can do anything with our emotions, we need to be aware of them. Some—like anger or fear—are more obvious, especially if we are experiencing them strongly. Others are more subtle, and we may not be consciously aware of them. Shame and guilt, for example, sometimes feel similar enough that it can be difficult for us to distinguish one from the other. Our ability to be aware of our emotions also depends on what we have been taught to do with them. If we were raised to believe that our emotions were bad and we needed to keep them under wraps at all times, we may have buried them so deeply that we have trouble accessing them. But access them we must. In this case, it is not a matter of what we don't know won't hurt us. Repressed emotions have and will continue to hurt us unless we bring them into our awareness and deal with them.

Anthony Robbins, in *Awaken the Giant Within*, talks about how our emotions serve us:

> The only way to effectively use your emotions is to understand that they all serve you. You must learn from your emotions and use them to create the results you want for a greater quality of life. The emotions you once thought of as negative are merely a call to action. Once you're familiar with each signal and its message, your emotions become not your enemy but your ally. They become your friend, your mentor, your coach; they guide you through life's most soaring highs and its most demoralizing lows.[1]

There are a number of techniques we can use that will help us to get in touch with our feelings. I will include some of these at the end of this chapter. Sometimes, however, if our feelings are repressed enough or resulted from a traumatic experience, we may need professional help to work with them. In this case, we may need the help of a professional therapist or a support group. For example, two international groups, The Mankind Project and Women Within, have been very effective at helping their members work through their emotions. Psychologists who are aware of these organizations often have referred their clients to these groups, believing in the work that they do and their ability to create a safe environment for accessing, exploring, and releasing emotions.

Getting to the Source of Our Emotions

Once we come to recognize and become aware of our emotions, we can work on getting to their source. When we react emotionally to a situation, often it is not the situation itself to which we are responding. The event is acting as a trigger, bringing up emotions we have experienced in the past. For example, if you were in a room with ten people and a speaker called the entire group stupid, you would all have different emotional reactions. Someone whose abusive father constantly berated him for being stupid when he was growing up might become totally enraged. Another person might feel some anger, but not nearly as much as the person with the abusive father. Yet another, who never experienced being called stupid, might not have any strong emotional reaction and wonder what caused the speaker to say such a thing.

Most of us spend far too much time living in our heads and too little in our hearts. We need to regularly monitor our feelings to see if we are living the life that we want for ourselves or that others have prescribed for us. In *Notes to Myself: My Struggle to Become a Person*, Hugh Prather states, "The more I consult my feelings during the day, tune in to myself to see if what I am doing is what I want to be doing, the less I feel at the end of the day that I have been wasting time."[2]

Our feelings do not lie. As humans we have an unlimited capacity to delude ourselves. Our minds, however, are unable to override our feelings. Our feelings always give us away and point out the inconsistencies in our life. Instead of tuning out our feelings, we need to get more in touch with them. To live an authentic, rewarding, and self-fulfilling life requires that we make use of both our intellect and feelings.

> "Become the change that you want to see in the world."
>
> —MOHANDAS GANDHI

> "Everyone thinks of changing the world, but no one thinks of changing himself."
>
> —RUSSIAN AUTHOR LEO TOLSTOY

Brad's Story

In his early forties, Brad's life had reached a crisis point. Dissatisfied with his job, he was convinced that what he needed was a change in careers. He suffered from constant fatigue and felt as if he were trapped in a rut from which he would never escape. Convinced that the job was his problem, Brad complained about his work to anyone who would listen. He was convinced that if he could only find more meaningful and fulfilling work, his life would get better. Tired of hearing his complaints, however, many of his coworkers found themselves avoiding him.

On the surface, Brad appeared to his coworkers and supervisor to be mild mannered and easygoing. He never showed signs of anger and seemed to handle stress on the job with ease. But beneath his calm and unflappable surface was a lot of pent-up frustration and anger. On occasions it would boil up. For example, a coworker sent an e-mail requesting that Brad do his job in a certain manner. Angry that he was being told how to do his job by someone with no authority over him, Brad wrote expletives on the message and sent it back to the coworker. Brad's supervisor called him in and questioned his behavior. Brad's boss told him that he could not understand why someone who was highly intelligent would act that way. This only made things worse as Brad started to notice that he was distancing himself more and more from those around him at work. Many of his coworkers avoided him and tried to avoid putting themselves in a situation where they would have to spend some time with him. Brad especially had problems with his direct supervisor, strongly resenting it anytime he was asked to do something. The supervisor was at the end of a long list of authority figures with whom he had problems.

Eventually, Brad realized that he was depressed, and had been so all of his life. When Brad became aware of his depression, he sought out professional help. Through counseling, he gradually began to delve into feelings that he had been avoiding for many years. The cause of his depression, he realized, had been the relationship he had with his father. He never felt good enough for his father, who frequently referred to him as an idiot. Even when Brad was well into his thirties, the father continued to belittle Brad in front of other people. Brad felt his father was a highly intelligent man who was bitter because he had never fully used his capabilities, but had worked in a menial job all of his life. As his self-awareness increased, Brad realized that he had picked up his father's life pattern.

During his counseling, Brad began to see all of the areas of his life that were impacted by his lack of awareness of his feelings. He realized that by not learning how to manage his feelings, he had been sabotaging his life. Besides seeing a counselor on a regular basis, he took in a lengthy session of group therapy. When Brad discovered ways he could release anger, he told those close to him that he felt real hope for the first time in his life.

Photography, which was always a serious interest in Brad's life, developed into a passion. Fear of rejection had kept him from entering his photographs in contests, even though several professional photographers had advised him to do so. Since entering, he has won a couple of awards for his photographs of nature. On Saturdays, he sells his photographs at a local market and finds it very satisfying having others appreciate his talents. At times, it is still difficult for him to accept that others are willing to pay money to have his work showcased in their homes.

Brad continues working in his same job, but claims things don't get to him as much as they used to. As his complaining about the job decreased, he found that coworkers no longer avoided him and for the first time he has been invited to parties by a number of colleagues. He has become friendlier and seems to have found a new interest in the people he is working with.

Although it is not the job of his dreams, Brad has come to the realization that it is not the worst job either and is noticing for the first time that there are some parts of his work that he really enjoys. Aware that his problems with authority figures stem from anger at his father, Brad has made an effort to build/develop respectful working relationships with his supervisors and managers at work.

Brad had an aha moment when he first came to the realization that his supervisor acted as a trigger for Brad's hostility, reminding Brad of his father. This awareness was the first step in repairing his relationships with his bosses. He made a conscious effort toward building a better relationship with them. While in the past he looked for differences that kept them apart, he now make a deliberate attempt to look for things that they had in common.

By taking an honest look at his feelings, and by committing himself to working with them, Brad turned his outlook around. He is now able to enjoy his life.

"You will have to leave the city of your comfort and go into the wilderness of your intuition. What you'll discover will be wonderful. What you'll discover will be yourself."

—ACTOR ALAN ALDA

Techniques for Increasing Emotional Self-Awareness

- **Take ten minutes every day.** Find a private place in which you are comfortable. Close your eyes and concentrate on your feelings. Be aware of tenseness in your body. Re-create events of the day that created some strong emotions. Try to re-create those emotions by remembering the events. At the end of the time, write down the different emotions you have identified in a book that you keep for this purpose. After a couple of weeks, notice if you are getting better at identifying emotions by the number you are able to re-create.

○ **If you have difficulty getting in touch with your emotions or have trouble telling them apart, see a therapist or join a group that specifically encourages you to express these emotions.** Sometimes seeing others get up the courage to share their feelings will trigger a desire in us to do the same.

○ **At the end of the day, if a strong negative emotion—such as fear, anger, or sadness—has come up, try to find the original source.** For example, if someone made you angry, ask yourself if that person reminded you of someone who made you angry in your past. Think back to the first time you were aware of experiencing that kind of anger.

○ **When you find yourself getting ready to react angrily, force yourself to not respond for at least ten seconds.** Have a thought ready—a pleasant memory or something that has puzzled you—that you force into those ten seconds. Do whatever works, whatever you have to do to force your mind to think about something else, but don't react.

○ **If you find yourself reacting from anger, fear, shame, or guilt, ask yourself afterward how you could have reacted differently.** After you have come up with a better way to handle the situation, concentrate on it for thirty seconds. Tell yourself that next time you will deal with it in this way.

○ **Every day look for an opportunity to share at least one positive emotion. Tell someone if something they did made you feel good.**

Notes

1. Anthony Robbins, *Awaken the Giant Within* (New York: Free Press, 1992), p. 249.
2. Hugh Prather, *Notes to Myself: My Struggle to Become a Person* (New York: Bantam Books, 1981), p. 17.

CHAPTER 6

Assertiveness

"Deliberate with caution, but act with decision; and
yield with graciousness, or oppose with firmness."

—CHARLES COLTON,
ENGLISH CLERGYMAN AND AUTHOR

A ssertiveness is the ability to maintain our boundaries and express our needs clearly and directly. It includes being able to express emotions that we are feeling and offer opinions that may be unpopular or run counter to the "group think." Although being assertive means asking for what we want, it does not mean we always get what we ask for. Assertiveness has gotten a bad rap in some areas of society because it is often confused with aggression.

Healthy assertive people, while being clear about their wishes, respect the rights of others. As much as assertive people maintain their boundaries, they respect the boundaries of others. Assertiveness allows for a difference of opinion without an attempt to beat the other person into submission or force them to come around to another way of thinking. It allows for a win/win situation, something that aggression does not. It is possible for two quite assertive people to maintain a close friendship and respect one another while disagreeing with each other. Often, people who stand up for their rights are respected for their actions, and are thought of more highly by others. However, since there is often a fine line between assertiveness and aggression, people who are respected are keenly aware of the boundaries of others and take great care to respect them.

Aggression

Aggression, on the other hand, demands winners and losers. The aggressor does not respect boundaries, and wishes to impose his or her will on the other party. Although aggression may achieve immediate goals, it leaves an ugly residue that will often come back to haunt the aggressor. The victim of aggression often feels bullied, resentful, and angry at the outcome and will often look for opportunities to undermine and "get back" at the aggressor. That is why aggressive people are generally resented and have few real friends. Although it may appear that they command respect, especially if they are in positions of power and authority over others, their hold on that respect is tenuous. The knives will be out should they fall from that position.

Passivity

While aggression is at one end of the standing-up-for-yourself scale, passivity is at the opposite end. Passive people are the proverbial doormats, letting others walk all over them. For whatever reason, passive people choose not to express their needs and desires and are often imposed upon by others. These people become victims in our society. Passive-aggression is another maladjusted place to be on the standing-up-for-your rights scale.

We all know people who are passive-aggressive. They appear quiet and undisturbed. Although it appears that they are going along with everything and nothing bothers them on the surface, underneath they are boiling, feeling the barb of every injustice that they perceive has been foisted on them. When finally they can't take it anymore, they explode with anger and rage. Passive-aggression is often a mechanism that is learned by people who are in vulnerable positions and have been punished for expressing their feelings and opinions. Often this behavior is learned in childhood when children learn that it is not okay to express anger or certain types of feelings, and their opinion doesn't matter. If they don't get help, the child will carry that passive-aggression into adulthood and use it with his or her spouse, superiors, friends, and others.

Adults, as well, can learn to bury their emotions and thoughts when they see no alternative to doing so, or when they are constantly beaten down for expressing them. Someone with an aggressive, overbearing boss or domineering partner may learn to keep their thoughts and feelings inside. When passive-aggressive anger finally boils over, it can cause a great deal of damage. Angry outbursts have often resulted in destroyed relationships, as well as lost friends and jobs. Career opportunities have often been severely curtailed or lost altogether, because of someone experiencing uncontrolled anger. It is crucial that passive-aggressive people learn to be assertive, to express themselves much earlier in situations than they feel the need to. This is behavior that can be learned with practice.

Healthy Assertiveness

There are as many effective ways to be assertive as there are personalities. While we have a vision of an aggressive person being loud and obnoxious, a quiet, soft-spoken individual can stand up for his or her rights as well as the outgoing and gregarious one. Teddy Roosevelt's maxim, "speak softly but carry a big stick," makes it clear that we are not to confuse quietness with lack of firmness and intent. Assertiveness requires an awareness of feelings and a good level of self-regard. We need to believe that our opinions and feelings matter before we will feel free to express them.

A certain level of independence is also important. The less dependent we are on the approval of others, the less fear we will have of offending them by being open, honest, and stating our wants. Because we usually can't blurt out the first thing that comes to our mind when someone says something contrary to our strongly held beliefs and values, a good measure of impulse control comes into play; otherwise we are apt to react out of anger or say something we will come to regret later. The person who manages to keep his or her cool in an angry and tense situation comes out the winner.

The world is full of people who will take advantage of us and cross our boundaries if we allow them to. To be able to make our own way and to get what we want out of life, we need to be able to consistently maintain our own boundaries.

"Firmness of purpose is one of the most necessary sinews of character, and one of the best instruments of success. Without it genius wastes its efforts in a maze of inconsistencies."

—PHILIP DORMER CHESTERFIELD, BRITISH STATESMAN

Don's Story

The topic of the workshop was "Making an Impact on the Job." More than forty participants had turned out to hear the speaker, who was billed as a leading expert on how to get noticed and advance in the workplace. His credentials were impressive. Don Maxwell had presented to large corporations, governments, and educators across the nation. He had been a guest on popular talk shows and drew a crowd wherever he went.

Don's delivery in front of the group was smooth and polished. He paused in all the right places to let his point sink in, and put emphasis on the areas he thought were important. Don stood tall, delivering his presentation with energy, enthusiasm, and confidence. He took turns making eye contact with all the participants, and made sure they all felt he was talking to them as individuals. His well-tailored suit, style, and demeanor all pointed to a man who was assured and successful. If any member of Don's audience were asked to imagine what the speaker's upbringing had been like, they would likely visualize a bright boy who had excellent grades, was good in sports, was popular with girls, and had the support of loving parents.

Their picture of Don's past could not be farther from the truth. Before he finished his presentation, Don asked his audience to try to imagine what his childhood and early adulthood had been like, based on what they had just seen and heard. At the end of the presentation, Don got personal and gave his audience a brief summary of his life. As a child he was skinny, awkward, and shy. His father, a tradesman, drank heavily. It was only later in life that Don learned that his father was an alcoholic. Although he was not abusive, he was totally absorbed in his own problems and had little to do with Don and his older brother Jason. The mother suffered from bouts of depression for periods of time. When she was feeling better, she was able to demonstrate affection for her sons, but when the depression hit her she withdrew into her own world. Don remembers feeling alone, frightened, and powerless, not having anyone in the immediate family to depend on during these times, except for his brother, who was only two years older.

There was one person they could rely on: Uncle Chuck on their father's side. Chuck was a war hero who had started his own business after the war ended and became quite successful. Even though he was only about five foot six, to the boys he was seven feet tall. Seeing that his nephews lacked parental direction, Chuck took them under his wing. Sensing Don's lack of self-confidence, he enrolled him in judo at the age of seven.

The class bully at his school had been picking on Don and some of the other smaller kids. With Chuck's encouragement, coaching, and judo training, Don finally worked up enough courage to fight back. He remembers the day clearly. He was walking down the hallway when the bully came up from behind and knocked his lunch bag out of his hand, spilling the contents on the ground. He then asked Don what he was going to do about it. Without giving it much thought, Don reached over and knocked the bully's books out of his hand, sending them skidding down the hallway. There was laughter from behind them. The bully, shocked and enraged, started to take a swing at the upstart. Don, expecting this, grabbed his arm and threw him to the floor. Shaken and hurting, looking stunned and quite sheepish, the goon slowly got up and walked away with his head down. He did not bother Don again.

Word spread quickly, and the shy, bullied kid became an instant hero, earning respect from both his classmates and teachers. While he was gaining self-confidence in taking care of himself physically, speaking up in public was another matter. Whenever the teacher asked a question Don froze, barely able to stammer out an answer in a weak, timid voice. When he told his uncle about his problem, Chuck proposed a plan. He told Don to visualize throwing the bully whenever he had to speak in public. He was to get a firm picture in his mind of being strong, confident, and sure of himself before starting to talk.

The first time he tried this, the teacher and other children in the class were silent for a moment, surprised by the strong and confident tone in Don's voice. The more he practiced the easier it got, and eventually the shy kid came to look forward to public speaking. He became confident enough in his own abilities that he ran for president of the students' union, finishing just behind the winner, the most popular girl in school and a beauty contest winner. Don was proud of his effort, knowing that he had given it his best shot. Uncle Chuck had always said that there was no shame in losing if he had done his best.

Don went to college and became a psychologist. Although he enjoyed helping people one on one, his passion was speaking to groups of people. At every opportunity he volunteered his speaking services to community groups and agencies. Although he wasn't making any money out of these activities, he saw them as an opportunity to hone his craft and gain valuable speaking experience.

Twenty years after graduating from college Don is a recognized speaker, specializing in staff development workshops and seminars. Although he no longer has to give free talks, he still volunteers to talk to school groups. Don loves to tell classes his "bully story" and sees himself in the faces of many of the quiet children sitting at the back of the class. His hope is that his message will give some of them the courage they will need to avoid becoming victims in life. He considers that even if his talk encourages them to do one thing they were afraid to try before, he will be successful. His theory is that once people stretch past their comfort point, they can never go back to the way they were.

Techniques for Increasing Assertiveness

- **Practice asking for what you want. Don't ask for permission or excuse yourself, just ask directly.** Tell yourself that your time and opinions are as valuable as anyone else's. Even if you don't really believe it, work up the courage and do it. Ask directly at least once per day. Start with situations less intimidating and work toward the more difficult ones.

- **Pay attention to the language you use.** Work toward cutting out pauses, "ahs," and "ums." These words are fillers and make you sound indecisive. Slow down speaking if you have to, but practice making your words sound firm and strong.

- **Call people by their first names, not their titles unless it is normal expected practice to refer to someone by their title (talking to your doctor).** Calling someone by a title when not called for gives them a position of power over you. Look people in the eye when talking to them.

- **Make it a habit to speak up and ask for compensation when you find something wrong with a purchase you have made, whether it is a meal in a restaurant, an item of clothing, or an auto repair.** Ask for evidence that work on your auto was done, such as seeing the old parts.

- **Don't let specialists intimidate you into not asking for clarification or explanation because you think they will see you as stupid.** It is up to them to simplify things so that you understand, not up to you to learn their technical expertise. Keep asking for explanations until you are comfortable and fully understand what they are saying.

- **Never speak up for yourself when you are feeling out of control, or anger will be clearly audible in your voice.** When you do this, you give the other person control over you. Wait until you can speak calmly and firmly. Remember, you are not attacking the other person, you are simply asking for what you want. If you don't get it, move on and try again. Focus on the fact that you were not afraid to try and did your best.

CHAPTER 7

Self-Regard

"Self-confidence is the first requisite
to great undertakings."

—BRITISH AUTHOR SAMUEL JOHNSON

"The man who has confidence in himself
gains the confidence of others."

—HASIDIC SAYING

S elf-regard is all about the way we see ourselves. It is an accurate assessment of the way we are, taking into account our strengths as well as recognizing our weaknesses. When most people hear the term *self-regard*, they think that it is synonymous with self-esteem. However, the originators of the BarOn EQ-i test have gone to great lengths to differentiate between the two. Self-esteem has been a buzzword for decades, and a lack of it was seen as the underlying problem for every person who had any form of dysfunction. The answer, therefore, was to boost people's self-esteem by telling them they were wonderful and deserving of respect for simply being who they were. It was thought that if we could raise people's self-esteem, they would be able to function more effectively.

This did not prove to be the case, however. It was often discovered after the fact that when we artificially increased someone's feeling of self-worth, we ended up with a dysfunctional person who felt good about the way he or she was. Not only did these people feel good, but they also saw little need to change, since they were fine just the way they were. This is clearly not the outcome that the social scientists who had worked on the concept of self-esteem had envisioned. The critical part that was missing was the requirement to achieve, to do something worthwhile in order to earn the right to feel good about oneself.

I mentioned earlier that we have an infinite capacity to delude ourselves, but that our feelings will always give us away. This seems to be the case with falsely inflating our self-worth. Deep down our feelings will not change, making our overblown image superficial at best. When I look back on my life, I see evidence that this is true. In high school I focused on my classes, seeing them as a first step to further education and to get to a place I wanted to be in my life. My marks were quite good, and in several courses I achieved top marks in the class. The principal made a statement, which I have never forgotten. He said, "Harvey, you have a good head on your shoulders, just don't let it go to your head." Accomplishments are something that you have to do for yourself and, as such, can never be taken away. They require dedication, courage, and hard work. They are an authentic source of self-regard. Our accomplishments need not be major, earth-shattering ones to give us a positive mental charge. Successfully completing any task that we see as difficult, or are not certain we can do, will give us a feeling of self-worth.

Certainly, getting my first book published gave me a powerful boost of positive energy. On a daily basis, I get all kinds of small boosts through doing everyday types of tasks well. For example, it makes me feel worthwhile every time I write a well-crafted letter or learn some useful new function on my computer. Whenever I do something for someone that they do not expect and receive sincere gratitude, I experience a positive feeling. Having the courage to try something can be gratifying even if it doesn't turn out the way we want. We will still come away with the satisfaction of knowing that we pushed ourselves beyond our comfort zone. I remember the feeling when actively dating of trying to work up the courage to call and ask someone out. The amount of courage required was directly proportional to how badly I wanted to go out with her, and how I estimated my chances of success. I would wait until the last minute to call for a date on the weekend, usually Wednesday night. Whenever I was turned down I had mixed feelings. On the one hand, I was disappointed that I didn't get a date. But I was also relieved that I had had the courage to call. The consequence of not being able to muster up enough courage to make the call was to never know what might have been. Making the call at least provided me with a sense of closure.

The only true failure in life is not having the courage to try. Whenever we stretch our comfort zone and risk ourselves in order to get something we want, our self-regard base increases. Look at it as a bank account. Instead of increasing our supply of money, we are increasing our supply of self-worth. The more we accumulate, the more opportunities we have to expand our lives. People who have healthy accounts of self-worth are always looking for growth opportunities. The larger our bank account becomes, the larger the opportunities after which we can go.

How do we know if people truly have a healthy amount of self-regard or are just faking it? We likely know people who have been quite successful, according to society's standards, even though they really don't feel good inside. There are many people who have succeeded because they have been clever enough to manipulate others and play the game well. However, people with high levels of real self-regard are supportive of others' goals and do not feel the need to put anyone down. They are supportive of the dreams and goals of other people and are not threatened by them. Forging ahead on their own path of personal discovery and growth, they welcome fellow travelers.

Southwest Airlines formed the CoHearts mentoring program to help new hires feel welcome. Employees volunteered to adopt and mentor newcomers and would be in constant touch with the newbies, buying them little gifts, taking them for lunch, and bestowing support upon them. As a result of this program, many close and supportive relationships were formed. Orientation day is a big deal, a cause for celebration. Typically, new employees are welcomed with a carnival-type atmosphere of balloons, confetti, music, and dancing. Lead by the chairman Herb Kelleher himself, groups of employees have been known to describe their jobs to the new hires while singing and dancing. At the end of the celebrations, balloons are often taken down to the airport waiting areas and given to children, creating a visual message of a company that really cares not only for its own people but for its customers.

> "Most powerful is he who has himself in his own power."
>
> —SENECA, ROMAN ORATOR AND WRITER

Monica's Story

Monica was raised in a strict family. Her father was very traditional, old-school, and believed that women did not need to have much education, as their role was to raise children and look after the house. Her mother was subservient to the father and did not support her daughter's dreams. The mother also believed that women were to serve their husbands and stay home to raise their children. Monica's two older brothers were encouraged to further their education. One went on to become an engineer and the other a pharmacist. Tall for a female at five feet nine inches and slender, Monica did not date much throughout high school. Although she was quite attractive, she tried to hide her attributes by dressing conservatively and wearing little makeup. Her marks were high enough that she could have been an honors student, but she deliberately got her lowest marks in religious studies. At the time she said she wasn't really conscious of why, but later came to realize that it was a way of rebelling against her parents, especially her father. Monica also excelled in sports, and became the star of her school's basketball team.

Despite her obvious talents, Monica did not feel good about herself. Lacking support from her parents, she didn't have any plans for the future. She did have one strong ally, however, her aunt Jennifer on her mother's side. Jennifer was a successful businesswoman who served as president of the local Chamber of Commerce. She had traveled all over the world on business and Monica looked up to her. Deep down, she sometimes wished that Jennifer were her mother. Her father did not approve of Jennifer, frequently criticizing her for her two failed marriages and insinuating she was a loose woman. Her mother did not defend her sister in front of her husband, but Monica detected in conversations with her that she was somewhat envious of Jennifer. Monica thought her father was also jealous of Jennifer, who was more successful financially than he was, better educated, and seemed to enjoy life a great deal more. Although her father objected, Monica began to spend more time with her favorite aunt. Jennifer was very supportive of her niece. Monica learned how to apply makeup and dress in ways that accentuated her natural beauty. With Jennifer's encouragement and financial support, she enrolled in dance classes. A naturally talented athlete, Monica found the dancing moves came to her fairly easily, and she started to thoroughly enjoy her new interest. It helped to increase her social interaction skills and her self-confidence.

Monica's aunt always reminded her that there would be people in her life who, out of petty jealousy and to make up for their own failures, would try to drag her down to their own level. She told Monica to avoid those people like the plague, but to get closer to people who appreciated her for who she was, and supported her. Monica took that advice to heart. When difficulties arose due to her situation at home, she would speak to her basketball coach and English teacher, both of whom were supportive and assured her that she had the ability to be anything that she wanted.

When she completed high school, Monica took a year off to work to save up some money and travel to Europe with a friend. Her father, as usual, was critical and unsupportive, going into a tirade about it being a waste of time and money. Her aunt however, liked the idea and encouraged Monica, telling her how much travel had increased her own sense of independence and knowledge, and broadened her outlook on life.

Coming from a sheltered background, Monica found her three months of traveling to be, as she describes it, "an awakening." She considers it one of the best things she did for herself, as it expanded her world and her self-confidence.

After her year was up, she decided that she wanted to become a teacher, specializing in physical education. She had her choice of a number of colleges and had no problem being accepted. The one she chose was several states from her home. At the beginning it was a struggle as she was away from home and missed her friends. However, she soon was busy with extracurricular activities as she tried out and was accepted on the college basketball team. It hurt whenever she heard her new classmates and friends talk about the support they were getting from their parents. She listened while they talked about going home to visit, or their parents coming up to see them. To Monica, these conversations were long and painful and she always felt a sense of relief when they moved to another topic. Monica's parents did not come to visit her and she seldom went home, except for holidays such as Thanksgiving, Easter, and Christmas.

Feeling like an outcast, she went to see a counselor at the college. The counselor allowed her to express her feelings and asked her to try to look at her situation in terms of a gift in which she turned her struggles into strengths. The fact that she was succeeding in life despite the obstacles in her way showed how strong, determined, and independent she was. She could be a role model to others in situations similar to hers, and would be sensitive to the kids she would teach who were going through what she had. Her struggles were character builders, giving her determination and endurance to carry on when things got tough. They would provide her with a solid foundation for building the rest of her life.

"I was thought to be 'stuck up,' I wasn't. I was just sure of myself. This is and always has been an unforgivable quality to the unsure."

—FILM STAR BETTE DAVIS

Techniques for Increasing Self-Regard

- **Run—don't walk—away from people who put you down or diminish you in any way.** Focus on spending time with people you know will be supportive. Do not delude yourself into thinking that you can bring negative people up. It won't happen; they will drag you down.

- **Make setting goals a part of your life.** Write them down and stick to them. Set goals for six months, one year, and five years. Make them achievable but hard enough that you will have to struggle to reach them. Become highly disciplined about this. I cannot overemphasize the importance of setting goals. If you need further motivation, ideas, and inspiration listen to motivational tapes by people like Anthony Robbins. They all talk about the importance of goal setting.

- **Keep a book of accomplishments.** Every week, pick one night and before you go to bed write down in that book everything you have accomplished that week. Don't forget personal things like bringing a smile to someone's face or making someone laugh. Think of things that made you feel good. If you have difficulty remembering an entire week, make a short list each night.

- **Ask people you trust and respect, and who know you well, to tell you what they see as your strengths.** Sometimes others are able to see attributes we have that we are not able to recognize.

- **Celebrate all of your accomplishments—small ones in a small way and big ones in a big way.**

- **Make it a habit to acknowledge other people's accomplishments and support them in the pursuit of their goals.**

CHAPTER 8

Self-Actualization

"You always pass failure on the road to success."

—MICKEY ROONEY, EMMY AWARD–WINNING AMERICAN
FILM ACTOR AND ENTERTAINER

"There is only one success—to be able to spend your
life in your own way."

—CHRISTOPHER MORLEY, AMERICAN JOURNALIST,
ESSAYIST, NOVELIST, AND POET

Self-actualization refers to what we have achieved in life compared with what we really want to accomplish. This is difficult to assess honestly and accurately. It requires us to be in tune with our true feelings and desires. Many people have long given in to other people's definitions of success, so that their own wishes have become buried in their subconscious. In our culture, we are programmed to immediately think of success in terms of how much we have accumulated financially and materially. Many people will see self-actualization strictly in terms of how well they have done in their careers or businesses, and how well they have managed their finances. Financial success can greatly enhance our freedom and expand our options in life, allowing us to enjoy and experience a much more varied lifestyle. As well, it can also give us a strong sense of achievement and increase our self-regard.

Success, though, is much broader than that, encompassing the whole of our lives, including our relationships with others, hobbies and interests, and our level of personal growth. There are people who have acquired much more than anyone expected of them, yet they are miserable, lacking good relationships with their families and others, and having no satisfying life outside of their work or business. But they are quick to find out that no amount of success will compensate for failure in our families.

> "This is the greatest time in history to be alive. This is the dawn of a new generation, the fully creative human being . . . the health seeking, prosperity attracting, relationship blessing and world transforming man and woman . . . the highest intelligence on Earth."
>
> —AUTHOR MARIANNE WILLIAMSON

The term *self-actualization* was originally coined by Kurt Goldstein, an organismic theorist who referred to the term as the motive for us to realize our potentials. The concept of self-actualization is usually associated with psychologist Abraham Maslow's hierarchy of needs theory. In this theory, there are different levels of needs, and we have to have our needs met in one area before we can move on to the next level. On the bottom level are the basic needs of food, clothing, and shelter. After that comes our need for safety. After our basic physical needs are met, we move on to emotional needs such as love and respect. On top of the hierarchy, at the peak of the pyramid, is self-actualization. Self-actualization is an embodiment of all of the higher human qualities such as the ability to form deep friendships, a sense of humor, independence, and autonomy. It is seen as the ultimate in human evolution to be able to transcend our environment instead of simply resigning ourselves to coping with it. Some people feel that this level can never be reached by humans. Nevertheless, it is a goal worth striving for. It is the ultimate of the human experience and unless we are actively striving for this we are selling ourselves short and settling for less than we can be.

Taking Your Life Where You Want It to Go

Self-actualization will be easier to determine for those who have had long-term goals in their lives and clear directions. Others, who have no clear path and have been unsure of where they wanted to get to in life, will have a more difficult time determining how far they have progressed on their journey. We assume that people who are rich and famous are following their dreams and have a sense of accomplishment in their lives. What they have is highly visible, and we are constantly reminded that this is what we should all strive for. Other kinds of achievement are much more subtle and hidden. For example, someone who has been on a long spiritual quest may feel that they have carried out their life's purpose. The only way we really know if we are living the life we are meant to live is to go inside. Since we have an unlimited capacity for deluding ourselves intellectually, our mind will not give us an accurate reading of how far we have traveled in our journey. Only our inner feelings will truly let us know if we are living the way we really want to.

We become what we think about. As discussed previously, our life today is a result of all of our thoughts from our past. One way to change the future is to think only of the things that we want.

The challenge is that experts tell us we have more than sixty thousand thoughts a day. It would be impossible to monitor our thoughts all day long to ensure that we are focusing on what we want from life. A powerful way to gain insight into our creative thoughts is to monitor our feelings. Our feelings are in sync with our thoughts. We cannot have negative thoughts and feel good and vice versa. Therefore if we are experiencing good feelings, our thoughts are on the right track. If we are experiencing stress, anger, or some kind of discomfort, our thoughts are negative and an indication to us that we are off course.

In his book *Flow: The Psychology of Optimal Experience*, Mihaly Csikszentmihalyi talks about a state of consciousness that we reach when we are totally absorbed in what we are doing. This state, which he calls flow, allows us to transcend our everyday problems and worries and feel that we have reached the pinnacle of our abilities. Csikszentmihalyi claims that we do not reach this ultimate state by chance, but by taking on tasks that are challenging but not above our abilities. Think of your life and see if there are times that you feel you have experienced flow.

My friend Julia experiences flow when she goes downhill skiing. When she is on top of her game and going through moguls, she feels like she could take off and fly. She feels like she is able to do anything. Her focus clears her mind and she becomes totally absorbed in her body and her skis. The skis become a part of her and she becomes the master of her universe. At the bottom of the slope, waiting for the lift to take her back up, Julia feels a warm afterglow, a feeling of total calm and comfort deep within herself.

Michel works as a head chef for one of the highest-rated restaurants in a major city. His articles have been published by major food and restaurant journals. When creating one of his award winning dishes, Michel appears to go into a trance. He jokingly says that his staff probably thinks that he has lost it as he has been told that he is so intense that he takes on the look of a madman. As he works on a dish, he imagines perfection and a total taste sensation every time a customer takes a bite of the dish.

Think about moments in your life when you were so totally engrossed in what you were doing that you forgot the time, or even where you were. What do you do that you are really good at, that you can really master? What challenges you in a way that is totally absorbing, that requires everything you have? These experiences of flow are signs on the highway toward self-actualization.

Inner Motivation

Our environment can support us in reaching our potential, or it can throw roadblocks and barriers in our way. Besides our own abilities, the type of environment we grow up in will determine which goals we feel are worth pursuing and which are not. Someone whose father is a wealthy, successful businessperson and who truly has the desire to be successful in business will receive much more support than someone who has the same amount of desire to be successful in business but happens to be the child of a single parent living on government assistance. Obviously, reaching the desired goal will require more inner resources for the latter person. It will require much more courage, perseverance, and dedication. People who leave their environment behind to go after their goals have to rely on feelings of inner satisfaction to motivate them. Often, their old environment will not applaud their progress, and their new world will not understand and appreciate their struggles from the perspective of where they are coming from. The saying that the acorn does not fall far from the tree is not always true. In some cases, it lands in an entirely different forest. The following is an example of someone who pursued a path far from his roots.

Ted's Story

Ted remembers growing up in a hardworking rural farm family, the youngest of three children. He has an older brother, who works in the trades. His sister works in an office in a small town close to where they grew up. Growing up, Ted always considered himself to be different from those around him. He often jokes that there must have been a mix-up at the hospital and he ended up going to the wrong parents. While other children in the local community were interested in the work of their parents and activities of the area, Ted was interested in world events. He consumed newspapers, articles, and books, while others his age were interested in tinkering with cars. Ted had no problem achieving good grades in high school, despite putting little effort into his work. He was naturally bright, had an excellent memory, and picked up new information very quickly.

In high school, while his male classmates planned to take over the family farm, take up a trade, or take a job in the local dairy processing plant, Ted considered becoming a teacher. He didn't really have an interest in teaching but thought it would give him a decent income and lots of time off during which he could pursue his other interests. At the time, he was not too sure of what he wanted to do, but he had already decided that it would not be in some traditional type of career.

When he was accepted into the education program at college, Ted found that he really enjoyed writing letters to his college paper. As a strong-willed person, he had definite opinions and no qualms about expressing those opinions. The more controversial the topic, the more Ted enjoyed writing about it. Although Ted enjoyed his college years, he already realized through his student teaching experience that this would not be the career for him. Despite this, he taught school for four years, counting the days until summer break and two months to do as he pleased. During those two months he traveled, keeping journals of his travels, envisioning travel writing one day in the future. At first, the reasons for Ted's unhappiness in teaching were not clear to him. He did enjoy teaching, liked the students, who seemed to enjoy his open, questioning style, and did not even mind marking papers. Although he was different from his colleagues in his approach to life, he was liked and respected. What he realized was that he needed to be independent in his work, to answer to no one but himself. He realized at this point that he did share one trait with his father, who had chosen to live in relative poverty as a farmer and be independent rather than to work for someone else.

When the time came to go back to teaching for the fifth year, Ted decided that he could take it no longer. Being conscientious with his money, he had managed to save enough to eke out a basic living for a year without working. He decided to take a year off, read, do some writing, and contemplate his future. As he was reading a popular book about stress, the thought occurred to him that it was quite boring and not that creative. Ted decided that he could write a better book on how to deal with stress. It took Ted six months to write his book. When he sent the idea off to publishers, he received rejection letters, one after another. Not a single publisher was willing to take a chance on an unknown author, even though some had written back that they found his ideas quite interesting. A friend from his college days, who had always wanted to write a book but did not seem to have any ability, came up with an idea. He would lend Ted the money if he wanted to self-publish. Ted promoted the book vigorously, getting himself on talk shows and doing interviews for newspapers. Sales of the book began to climb and within six months Ted's friend had his money back plus a nice little sum for his faith in Ted's abilities.

In the meantime, Ted continued to use every minute of his time to promote and plan his next book. With book sales in the respectable range for a first-time author, Ted again approached publishers with a proposal for another book. This time, after the usual string of rejection letters, he finally found a publisher who was interested. His first book was now becoming quite well known and Ted was receiving requests to do talks and presentations. Drawn by the fun and easy reading style of his book, associations and organizations began to ask him to do presentations to their staff. During the next couple of years, Ted was very busy writing and giving presentations. Drawing from the momentum created by his first book, Ted's next book had strong sales as well.

Ten years later, Ted continues to write and deliver presentations. He now has seven books published, five that have been published in various foreign countries as well as North America. His lectures have taken him across North America, and he has been to Europe several times. In slow periods, between lectures and finishing another book, Ted spends time in one of his favorite destinations such as Bali or Mexico. Many people whom he knows envy his lifestyle and success. While he acknowledges that he had a few lucky breaks along the way, he feels that success came about due to his belief in himself and relentlessly focusing on and working toward his goals. His next goal is to get a book on the *New York Times* best-seller list. According to Ted, some days his life seems like he is living out an episode of *Fantasy Island*. It's not perfect yet, and he expects it never will be. Self-actualization to Ted is a road, not a destination. To him, the essence of life is setting goals and striving to reach them. He philosophizes that if we reached all of our goals, life would lose its zest and energy, and would stop being worthwhile.

"What's money? A man is a success if he gets up in the morning and goes to bed at night and in between does what he wants to do."

—MUSICIAN BOB DYLAN

"If your success is not on your own terms, if it looks good to the world but does not feel good in your heart, it is not success at all."

—AUTHOR ANNA QUINDLEN

"The penalty for success is to be bored by the people who used to snub you."

—NANCY ASTOR, FIRST WOMAN TO SIT AS AN MP
IN THE BRITISH HOUSE OF COMMONS

"Success usually comes to those who are too busy to go looking for it."

—HENRY DAVID THOREAU, AMERICAN AUTHOR,
NATURALIST, AND PHILOSOPHER

Techniques for Increasing Self-Actualization

- **Think of the things that are the most important in your life.** They can be work, family, leisure, hobbies, or spirituality. You may have to dig deep to find these things. Be brutally honest with yourself: what do you really want? (not what someone else expects of you). Make a list of the three most important things.

- **Create goals around the top three most important things in your life.** Do you want to reach a certain level in your career? Do you want a closer relationship with your spouse and children? Do you want to travel the world? Set measurable, specific goals around those three areas. Set goals for a month, six months, one year, and five years. Set aside a specific time for reviewing those goals. I review my goals every spring and fall during a trip to the mountains that I plan for that specific purpose.

○ Mark into your day-timer, or however you keep track of your daily activities, five minutes to do nothing but think about your goals.

○ Listen to motivational tapes at every opportunity, driving to work or during your spare time.

○ Ask someone close to you to remind you periodically of your goals and give you feedback on how much progress you are making.

○ **Never share your goals with anyone who is not supportive, or even whom you expect may not be supportive.** Share your most powerful, far-reaching goals only with an intimate circle of people whom you are close to and will be totally supportive.

CHAPTER 9

Independence

"Self-reliance is the only road to true freedom, and
being one's own person is its ultimate reward."

—Author Patricia Simpson

Independent people constantly strive to be masters of their own destiny. They prefer to think and make decisions on their own path rather than follow the prevailing way of thinking and allowing others to decide for them. Yes, they do consider other people's opinions and take into account the information provided to them. In the end, however, they settle on what works best for them. Independent types can sometimes be misunderstood and accused of being arrogant or not being good team players. They are neither; they are just marching to the beat of their own drummer. People who have a high degree of independence are free of emotional dependency. They will not stay in a relationship or a job that does not meet their needs for long.

Individuality vs. Community

We have inherent needs to be both ourselves and at the same time part of something larger, a community. These two often opposing needs are one of the dichotomies of life that we all struggle with. Healthy, functioning individuals have managed to find a balance between maintaining a strong sense of who they are and giving of themselves for the good of the community.

All relationships require a degree of mutual dependency. There is an inherent conflict in being part of a couple between each person being themselves versus being part of a couple. It is a normal dynamic and one that has to be dealt with in any relationship. In healthy relationships this is dealt with openly and honestly and both partners learn to grow more secure in their relationship while still maintaining and growing their individuality. In essence, as each person grows as an individual, he or she has more to give to the relationship. As each person grows, so does the relationship. This is called interdependence.

On the other hand in a codependent relationship, individual growth is viewed as a threat to the relationship by one or both of the parties. Issues are seldom openly dealt with and one partner often tries to intimidate or bully the other. It is based on fear and insecurity that one of the partners will leave the relationship.

In the workplace as well as in the home, interdependence is the key to a successful relationship. Like in any familial relationship there is an inherent ongoing struggle between what is good for the employee and what is good for the organization. Employees who feel that they are able to grow themselves in their place of business will have more to offer the organization. Their newfound skills and confidence will be paid back to the organization in terms of increased productivity and loyalty to the organization. Southwest Airlines has managed to produce a workplace environment that is highly conducive to interdependency. Staff members are encouraged to retain and grow their individuality while at the same time increasing their loyalty and value to the organization. In the end, it is a win-win situation whereby the individual is able to reach his or her own potential while at the same time belonging to and contributing toward a supportive community.

Independent types do not have the same urge to fit in or be popular as their more dependent cohorts. They are driven more by their internal forces than by the expectations of society or others around them. Being independent requires a good dose of self-regard as well as courage. Independence requires taking risks and living with the results of things not turning out as hoped. This is all part of the price that has to be paid for making one's own way in life. It is also part of the learning curve for autonomous types, as they learn from their mistakes, forgive themselves, and move on. Believing in oneself is a necessary prerequisite for independence, as there will be times when decisions will have to be made without a lot of support and backing from others.

There are many well-known examples of individuals who have persevered despite many setbacks before they reached their goal. Abraham Lincoln did not simply become president overnight. He tried and failed many times while running for public office before he reached the pinnacle of his success. Thomas Edison was unsuccessful thousands of times in his attempts to build an electric lightbulb. The papers of the day were printing articles ridiculing his project, calling it foolishness and admonishing him to give up and admit defeat. A young reporter interviewing him asked him why he persisted in this folly when it was clear that he was not getting anywhere. He told the reporter that he did not understand failure. Failure was not what it appeared to be for most people, but rather the price that had to be paid for success. Edison went on to say that every time he failed he could eliminate one way of doing it, bringing him one step closer to the way that would work. Obviously, Lincoln and Edison had to have a great deal of internal motivation and a high degree of self-worth to withstand external judgments and pressures.

Independence also requires a certain amount of assertiveness. Independent people are not afraid to ask for what they want, and do not give up if they do not immediately get what they are after. They usually are not afraid to try new things and pursue a diverse range of interests. To be happy and fulfilled, independence-oriented individuals need to find partners and workplaces that will accommodate and support their needs. Many work for themselves or are in positions that allow them a great deal of flexibility in their roles. Independent people realize that they have to find either an environment in which they can reach their potential or else create one for themselves. They are not afraid to leave an employer who will not give them opportunities to make the most of their talents. In *Successful Intelligence*, Robert Sternberg talks about the need for people to make the most of what they have.

There is a story of a man who dies and goes straight to heaven. Saint Peter gives him a brief tour of the premises and points to an individual, mentioning that he was the greatest poet of his time. The man looks at Saint Peter, incredulous. "Excuse me," he says, "but I knew that man. He was nothing more than a humble shoemaker. He never even went to school or learned how to write." "Precisely so," responds Saint Peter. Never given the chance to develop his writing skills, the man's prodigious talent went to waste. The story would be more humorous if it weren't true of so many people.

Successful intelligent people realize that the environment in which they find themselves may or may not enable them to make the most of their talents. They actively seek an environment where they can not only do competent work but also make a difference. They create their own opportunities rather than let their opportunities be limited by the circumstances in which they happen to find themselves.[1]

"Depend not on another, but lean instead on thyself. True happiness is born of self-reliance."

—THE LAWS OF MANU

Laura's Story

Out of high school, Laura got a job working as an operations coordinator for a tour company in Alaska for the summer. The atmosphere of Alaska—the freedom of the open spaces and independent spirit of the people who lived there—suited her. The job was not an easy one. She had to give direction to a group of male tour bus drivers, who were almost all older than she was and some of whom had worked for the organization for a number of years. Although some staff members resented her, others admired her for being able to stand on her own two feet.

Although Laura enjoyed her independence, she also found that it came with a price. She found herself at times left out of social gatherings that most of her coworkers were invited to. Sometimes she caught herself thinking that she had become too independent and would not fit in with coworkers who all appeared to be needier than she was. At times she felt lonely and unsupported. To counter this feeling, she began to ask for advice from coworkers more and made it a point to thank others for their input even though she only acted on it occasionally. Over time, she found her coworkers became more open and warm with her. At times, she wished she was less independent and more like everyone else. However, she decided that there were trade-offs in life and maybe not being one of the in crowd was a price that self-sufficient souls like her had to pay. Her boss valued her ability to think and act independently and trusted her judgment to make sound decisions. The business was growing quickly, decisions had to be made quickly and on the spot, and he needed people who were able to do so. Besides being independent, Laura was good at problem solving and able to think on her feet. She was confident in her abilities and had good empathy. She used her strong people skills to soothe disgruntled customers.

Laura understood her strengths and encouraged Dan, her boss, to let her handle more responsibility in areas that she thoroughly enjoyed and was highly competent in. Because his operations were overstretched, Dan was happy to give Laura plenty of leeway because he had faith in her.

One of the staff members whom Laura supervised in her office was Jennifer. Her shyness and lack of faith in her own decision making reminded Laura of herself when she was growing up. She spent extra time with Jennifer, asking her to think of a couple of solutions to the problems that she typically came to Laura with. Most of the time, they were not decisions that would have drastic consequences if they were wrong. Whenever Jennifer came up with a decision, Laura told her to go ahead and do it. If the decisions ended up being the wrong choices, Laura turned it into a learning experience, asking Jennifer what she would do differently. At the end of each discussion, she always stressed that Jennifer had made the best decision with the information she had at the time and that every wrong decision was an opportunity for growth and learning.

At times, Laura found herself becoming impatient and wanting to scream at Jennifer. She was careful, however, not to show her frustration when they were together, knowing that if she did any progress she was making, even if it seemed at times to be very little, would be lost. After several months, Laura noticed that Jennifer was approaching her less with routine decisions that she was quite capable of making herself. Usually when she now came to Laura, she was in over her head and needed Laura's advice. Instead of simply making a decision for Jennifer, Laura would talk over the situation, give Jennifer the benefit of the information she had and ask Jennifer what she would do. She always made sure that Jennifer had some part in the decision-making process.

Through her job, Laura met an operations coordinator for another tour company. She and Ed enjoyed a lot of things together—canoeing, hiking, and camping in the mountains. Both were active and stayed in shape. Since Ed was also highly independent, it seemed like a match made in heaven. Deeply in love for the first time in her life, they were married six months later. After the honeymoon, it did not take Laura long to realize there was a side to Ed that she had noticed but, in her state of bliss, had chosen to ignore.

Although he was independent himself, he had a great deal of trouble accepting her independence. It was a threat to him and he was opposed to anything new that she wanted to try. She described him as a control freak who needed to dominate every detail of her life as well as make all decisions that should have been made jointly in a healthy relationship. It was a difficult time for Laura. For the first time in her life, she began to have serious doubts about herself and her self-worth suffered. Ed continually told her that she was abnormal and had problems. It began to dawn on Laura that she was in a codependent relationship. As much as she tried to reassure

Ed about their relationship, she realized that she had very little control over his insecurities. After two years, Laura had had enough and they were divorced.

It took her about six months to get back to where she had the confidence to go out and do things on her own. One day she realized that it was sure great to have the old Laura back again. Her independent spirit was challenged, but had resurfaced and she was excited to think of the possibilities to come.

"It requires greater courage to preserve inner freedom, to move on in one's inward journey into new realms, than to stand defiantly for outer freedom. It is often easier to play the martyr than to be rash in battle."

—AMERICAN PSYCHOLOGIST ROLLO MAY

Techniques for Increasing Independence

○ **At the end of the day, write down a decision that you made on your own in a notebook you keep just for that purpose.** It is okay if you sought input from others to gather information and help you decide, as long as you did not expect others to decide for you.

○ **Practice making quick decisions on small, unimportant matters.** When looking at a menu in a restaurant, for example, give yourself three minutes to make a decision. Ask someone to time you or time yourself. Stick to the time limit.

○ **Every week do one thing for yourself, by yourself.** Choose something you always wanted to do but were afraid to, or did not want to do alone. For example, did you want to go to a certain movie but couldn't find anyone to go with? Go on your own this week.

○ **When in a group, do you speak up and voice an opinion if it is different from the others? If not, do so this week.** Force yourself to speak up and say how you really feel. Think about it after and tell yourself that you're glad you had the courage to speak your mind, even if the others did not support it. Do this the following week and the week after that.

o **If you are always going out for lunch with the crowd at work, try going alone once per week.** Choose a place different from the usual place you go. Try a different type of food. Explore.

o **Sit down and look at changes that you want to make to your life.** Be honest with yourself. Make a list of what you want to change in a month, six months, and one year. Write them down and put in specific things you need to do by a certain time. Stick to your plan. If you miss a step, go back and start again. Set aside a specific time to look at your plan annually. Reward yourself for meeting your goals. Set the rewards to match the goals. Celebrate major goals with major rewards, such as a trip, stereo system, or whatever else you can afford but have denied yourself.

Note

1. Robert Sternberg, *Successful Intelligence* (New York: Simon & Schuster), p. 2.

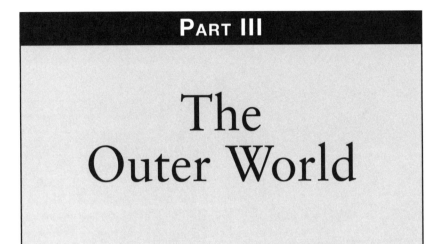

PART III

The Outer World

CHAPTER 10

Empathy

"The great gift of human beings is that we have the power of empathy."

—Actress Meryl Streep

There are people who can understand others, while some people have absolutely no idea where others are coming from. Even though we may not be consciously aware of it, we naturally feel closer to people who understand us and therefore tend to become more open and trust them. Think of the people you go to for support and comfort when you need it. What qualities do they have? They are people with empathy.

Empathy means being able to accurately read where other people are at emotionally. It means being able to get below the words others are saying to sense the underlying feelings. To do that, we must be able to pick up not only the words but also the force and tone with which they are said. Along with this, we also need to take into account facial expression, posture, and other indicators that will give us valuable clues into the person's emotional state.

Empathy Is Not Sympathy

There is a lot of confusion about what empathy is. For some people, it has warm and fuzzy connotations and words like *warm, sympathetic,* and *caring* come to mind.

But empathy does not mean we necessarily have to express ourselves in a warm, caring, or sympathetic way. Empathy is often confused with sympathy but the two are quite different. Sympathy brings out our own feelings. When we feel sorry for someone, we are not in the best state to be doing what is best for that person. Let's say, for example, that someone close to us whom we care a great deal about is injured and has to learn to live with a handicap. We watch the person struggle to do tasks that were simple before, but since the accident have become quite difficult. In order for that person to become independent again, however, it is essential that he learns how to do these types of things for himself. If we feel sympathy for the person, we might feel compelled to rush in and help with the task. This would not do the person any favors, however, since it would delay his ability to learn to do the task himself and impede his progress toward becoming independent. Our empathy, on the other hand, would allow us to see the situation that the person is in, yet step back and act in a manner that would ultimately be in that person's best interest.

I remember going bowling with my nephew Brett when he was in his preteens. He wanted more than anything to beat his Uncle Harvey. As much as I wanted to throw a game to let him win, I felt that it would not benefit him unless he was able to win a game fair and square. I knew that at some point he would be able to beat me and eventually he did. At that point he was able to savor a true, authentically earned victory. Letting him win before that would have denied him this experience.

Having received training in one of the helping professions, my professors went to great lengths to explain the difference. In helping relationships, getting hooked into someone's feelings causes us to lose our objectivity along with the ability to help the person. Not only that, it results in pretty rapid burnout.

We do not have to feel sorry for other people, or relate our own feelings to theirs to understand how others are feeling. Empathy allows us to imagine how the world would look like through someone else's eyes, yet at the same time not be drawn in emotionally to their realm.

In their revised and updated version of *The EQ Edge: Emotional Intelligence and Your Success*, authors Steven J. Stein, Ph.D., and Howard E. Book, M.D., define empathy as:

The ability to see the world from another person's perspective, the capacity to tune in to what someone else might be thinking and feeling about a situation—regardless of how that view might differ from your own perception. It is an extremely powerful interpersonal tool. When you make an empathic statement, even in the midst of an otherwise tense or antagonistic encounter, you shift the balance. A contentious and uneasy interchange becomes a more collaborative alliance.[1]

Empathy happens at an awareness and understanding level. We do not have to agree with people or particularly like them to have empathy for them. Think about someone you really don't care for. Imagine that person losing someone very close to them. Although we might not feel sympathy for the individual, we can understand the feelings of grief and loss the person would be going through.

Empathy is one of the key ingredients that successful salespeople possess. Many people see sales as being all about giving the customer the best deal, the best product, and service at the best price. But selling is primarily about relationship building. Spend some time thinking about salespeople from whom you made major purchases. Why did you decide to buy from these individuals? Did you like them? This may seem like a silly question and an oversimplification, but think about an instance when you bought something substantial from someone you didn't like. Most likely you haven't.

Most people think of life insurance in terms of costs and benefits. Traditionally, salespeople in that field were taught that in order to make a successful sale you had to convince the customer that your policy was better than your competitor's. American Express brought in consultants trained in emotional intelligence to help their life insurance sales force become more effective. From the consultants they discovered that selling life insurance involved much more than facts and figures. When we think of our own demise and loved ones we are leaving behind, a lot of emotions come into the equation. Salespeople who are sensitive to this and able to effectively demonstrate this sensitivity to their customers sell more life insurance policies.

Putting Empathy to Work

Fiona was Corrie's manager at a branch of a large financial institution that had branches across the United States, Europe, and Asia. They had recently come up with a new process that Fiona was hoping that the organization would adopt throughout their operations. As Corrie was instrumental in developing the process and was a recognized expert on the topic in her branch, Fiona decided she would be the natural choice to present to the annual meeting of the U.S. division. Although Corrie was very knowledgeable, she was somewhat of an introvert and not comfortable speaking to large numbers of people. The annual meeting would have up to four hundred employees from various levels from all across the country. She met with Fiona to discuss her concerns and anxieties concerning the presentation.

Corrie: I'm not really good with talking to a lot of people. I get really nervous and have trouble concentrating on what I have to say. I wish someone else could do the presentation.

Next are three examples of how Fiona could have responded, indicating varying levels of empathy.

Response 1

Fiona: You'll do fine. There's nothing to it. You know this stuff better than anyone else around here.

In this response, Fiona showed a complete lack of empathy. She failed to even acknowledge Corrie's anxiety over the presentation, which would be the first basic step toward working on a solution with her. Instead, she dismissed Corrie's feelings entirely, leaving Corrie even more anxious and feeling completely unsupported and misunderstood.

Response 2

Fiona: Lots of people have a fear of public speaking. I used to until I went to Toastmasters. Now I'm okay, even though I get a little nervous. There's nothing wrong with being a little nervous. You know your stuff well, so you'll be okay.

In the second response, Fiona at least acknowledged Corrie's anxiety. She did not address it, however, only speaking about it in general terms and talking about her own experience. She did not invite Corrie to help her look for ways to lesson her anxiety. As a result, Corrie still feels that her concerns were not taken seriously and addressed in a caring manner.

Response 3

Fiona: Sounds like you are feeling really stressed over the thought of having to do this presentation.

Corrie: Yeah, I get knots in my stomach and tongue-tied when I have to talk in front of a group of people.

Fiona: Sounds like you are really stressed out about this presentation. I remember feeling like that up to a couple of years ago whenever I had to present something. Since I started going to Toastmasters, I've been able to shed a lot of my anxiety, although I still get a bit nervous. Have you ever considered going to something like Toastmasters? It really helped me.

Corrie: I probably should. I've heard good things about it. A friend of mine has been with them for five years and always wants to take me as a guest. This presentation is only a couple of weeks away and Toastmasters won't help me this time.

Fiona: Is there anything I or anybody else on the team could do to help? Would it help if you did a trial run at our unit meeting this Thursday? You don't have any problems talking to our group and it might help you feel more confident. If you want I can set up a meeting with Garret in communications. I hear that he has some good exercises that you could work on that might take off some of that anxiety load that you're carrying. If you want more practice, I can talk to the folks in unit C about practicing your presentation at their unit meeting next Thursday. You know all of them pretty well and the more you practice, the more comfortable you'll become. That's the way it's always worked for me anyway.

Corrie: Sure, I'll give it a try. Maybe once I've done it a few times in front of people I'll feel better.

In this instance, Fiona showed good empathic listening skills. She responded directly in a caring manner that indicated that she understood where Corrie was coming from. Corrie felt that she was heard, understood, and cared about. Having been in Corrie's shoes, she used this to build trust and understanding for working toward a solution that they both could live with. She explored with Corrie some ideas that might help her get the fear monkey off her back, or at least lighten his weight.

It would have been even better if Fiona had let Corrie come up with her own solutions to her anxiety. In this case, Fiona felt that Corrie's anxiety would limit anything she could come up with on her own. Besides, time was running out and they did not have the luxury of a long-term plan. Overall, it was an effective use of empathy. Chances are Corrie will become more confident and will do a good job in the presentation. She knows she has the support of her boss and coworkers and her relationship with Fiona has become stronger. If things go well, she will come away feeling more self-confident. She may also feel grateful to Fiona for believing in her enough to not take the easy way out and give the presentation to one of her coworkers.

A company that exudes empathy is Southwest Airlines—from management to the employees and employees to one another. Lorraine

Grubbs-West, an executive with the company, describes what happened when her husband became ill with cancer.

> My husband had been ill with cancer for over two years and everyone in the system had provided *incredible* support. Baskets of cards from people across the company dotted the landscape inside my home and many had even *given me their vacation days* so I could spend time with my husband at the hospital! At three o'clock sharp, a huge black limousine pulled up in front of our home and the entire staff from my office piled out! Excitedly, they explained that they were inviting me and my family to dinner at a five-star restaurant and then to see a performance of *A Christmas Carol*. It was the middle of December, and we had a marvelous family evening—one I will never forget. It would also be the last meal my husband was able to eat. He passed away just a few weeks later.[2]

The Power of Acknowledging Feelings

One day at a local park, I ran into my friend Linda and her two grandchildren, six-year-old Josh and his ten-year-old brother, Warren. The brothers had a close relationship, apart from the usual squabbles that boys their age get into. Things were going well until Josh started crying. Between sobs he complained bitterly to his grandmother that his older brother had said something to him or done something that he did not like. Linda reacted quickly. "Josh, I know you have to cry because you feel hurt, but if it doesn't stop in five minutes you're going to have to go sit in the car."

I have seen many situations in which a six-year-old starts crying, so I expected a long and drawn-out episode of tears and wailing. This is often accompanied by the parent raising their voice and threatening consequences if the child does not stop. The more the parent threatens, the more the child cries. It becomes a standoff, a power struggle of sorts.

Therefore, I was quite shocked to see that after a few more sobs, Josh stopped crying and muttered "okay." This seemed quite amazing. What special skills did Linda have that could get a six-year-old to stop crying, and so quickly? She simply used a basic understanding of feelings and how they affect us. There are four basic rules about feelings.

1. Feelings are neither good nor bad, they just are.
2. We are all entitled to our feelings.
3. We have no right to judge other people's feelings and nobody has a right to judge ours.
4. We all have a strong need to have our feelings acknowledged.

Linda's acknowledgment of Josh's feelings resulted in his being able to let go of them easily and quickly. There was no longer any need to hang on to them. Within a few minutes, he and Warren were engaged in a game, the incident forgotten. Linda's other message to Josh was that, while his feelings were okay and natural, there was a time to express them and a time to move on. To continue to express them after that time would not benefit him.

"Friendship is a living thing that lasts only as long as it is nourished with kindness, empathy, and understanding."

—AUTHOR UNKNOWN

Susan and Tanya's Story

Susan was responsible for her sister Tanya, who was five years younger. Susan took on a great deal of the parent role by looking after her younger sister at an age when she was still a child herself. Her father was very controlling and demanded that Susan look after her little sister whenever the parents weren't around. Years later, Susan was to find out from an uncle that her father had been made by his parents to be responsible for a younger brother and this was a continuation of a family cycle.

Ever since she could remember, Susan had been afraid of her father. He saw himself as the rightful head of the household, was demanding of his family, and was intolerant of any sign of weakness. Her mother, submissive and withdrawn, turned over all parental decision-making and discipline issues to her dominant husband.

Although not as harsh as he was, inevitably Susan became a model of her father, expecting the same kind of behavior from Tanya as her father expected from her. Tanya resisted what she felt was her older sister's controlling of her life and constantly telling her what to do.

A free spirit with a propensity for rebellion, Tanya was constantly getting into mischief, doing things that she shouldn't. Susan was constantly blamed for the trouble Tanya was in because she wasn't watching her sister as closely as she should have. Susan carried the hurt and sense of gross unfairness that she was punished for something that Tanya did into adulthood. Susan, always the responsible one, went on to university and obtained a degree in personnel administration with honors. From there, she went on to become a manager in a large company. Tanya, always the free spirit, worked at various jobs after completing high school and traveled the world, working at different places. After bouncing around for a number of years all over the world, Tanya applied to and was accepted into a journalism course at college. Talented and not afraid of taking risks, the field suited Tanya perfectly. After graduating, she found work with a major media outlet and excelled at her job. In her personal life, however, she continued to harbor a great deal of anger at the way Susan had treated her growing up. She seldom called her sister, who was the only one who made an effort to stay in touch.

Susan had a great deal of anger at both of her parents—at her father for his harshness and unfair treatment of her, and at her mother for not fulfilling her responsibilities as a parent. Eventually, she joined a women's self-help group where she was encouraged to vent her feelings and share them with the rest of the group. This helped Susan a lot. The intensity of the anger and the duration were a lot less than before.

Susan's next step was to share her story with Tanya and hope that her younger sister would be able to forgive her. In the past, all of Susan's attempts to draw Tanya into conversation about their childhood resulted in Tanya getting angry, yelling at Susan, and calling her a tyrant. This was hard for Susan to accept, but she was determined to keep on trying to reach out to her sister.

When she phoned Tanya the next time, she was surprised by the tone of Tanya's voice. It did not sound angry or resentful. Susan was surprised to learn that Tanya herself had joined a women's self-help group and was working through some issues. Although she sounded a little guarded, Tanya agreed to spend a weekend with Susan. They went away to a cabin in the mountains. "It was like a cleansing process," said Susan. "We talked, cried, talked, and cried some more."

Susan told Tanya she understood how she felt toward her. She shared her feelings about those times with Tanya, such as how much pressure she felt from their father and how it felt to be punished for something that Tanya did. Susan listened while Tanya talked about what it was like to have Susan on her case all the time, how smothered and controlled she felt.

Both of them came away with an understanding of why the other acted and behaved the way she did. Sharing their feelings was the first step in the long process of building a relationship. Although the road ahead was still long and hard, both had taken the first giant step on the journey and things between them had changed forever.

After the weekend, both Tanya and Susan became more aware of how the relationship between them and their parents was playing itself out in various scenarios in their workplaces. Susan became aware that she was often short and impatient with subordinates whom she felt she had to coddle and handhold. Susan realized that she had been micromanaging her staff, unconsciously playing the big sister role, which was expected of her by her father, in the workplace. Only after the weekend with her sister was she able to begin breaking free of the urge to babysit her employees.

Giving back more control of their work to Susan's staff was not easy. Several had become quite dependant on her and looked quite anxious the first time she told them that she trusted them and did not have to always check their work. When they came to her with a question, she would ask them to come up with a possible solution before coming to her. Over time, Susan was able to wean them off of the dependency that she herself had contributed toward creating.

As her relationship with Tanya evolved over time, Susan used her as a sounding board to talk about work situations. Tanya's feedback was valuable as she was able to see things from the viewpoint of Susan's staff. While her staff were often too afraid or timid to tell her exactly how they felt about her, Tanya was able to offer her version of what they might be experiencing. It took some time, but slowly Susan saw signs that she was beginning to trust her employees.

Tanya had her own issues at work. Always a free spirit and independent, she bristled at the thought of being told what to do. Anyone in the position of authority over her—including Sabrina, the senior editor—was the object of her subtle and on occasion overt hostility. Tanya had a column in a major paper and even though she worked independently a great deal, Sabrina had to approve her work and at times request that she make changes. Tanya, however, did not appreciate these suggestions, taking them as criticisms. Tanya gave her the cold treatment whenever Sabrina gave her feedback on her writing.

After the weekend with her sister, Tanya had her own awakening. She realized that Sabrina strongly reminded her of her older sister. The more she seriously thought about it, the more she began to realize that she had been unfair to her boss. While her boss had meant feedback to be constructive and helpful, what Tanya heard was the criticism from an older sister. She felt some guilt over having treated Sabrina this way and at times felt that she had been acting like a spoiled brat. Deciding that she needed to do something to make amends to her boss, she asked her to go for lunch.

At first lunch was tense, with Sabrina sensing that Tanya was struggling with something she wanted to say but wasn't sure how to start. Tanya suddenly started crying and it all came pouring out. It all came out jumbled, about her older sister, the weekend, how she realized that she had been "a real bitch" to Sabrina and she was sorry as she "did not deserve to be treated that way." After she stopped crying, Sabrina went up to her and gave her a big hug. This was better than she had expected. It was a giant first step toward a long and fulfilling work relationship.

"We feel most comfortable around those that we sense, at some level, are most sensitive to our needs and feelings. We also tend to trust them more. . . . The really important things are not houses and lands, stocks and bonds, automobiles and real estate, but friendships, trust, confidence, empathy, mercy, love, and faith."

—BERTRAND RUSSELL,
BRITISH PHILOSOPHER AND HISTORIAN

Techniques for Increasing Empathy

○ **Every day pick a conversation and pay attention to the feelings behind the words.** Also pay attention to the tone of the words. Ask a question or two about the feelings to see if your perceptions are accurate.

○ **When a group of people are having a conversation and you are not directly involved, try to figure out how each person is feeling by paying attention to tone of voice, facial expressions, and words with underlying meanings.**

○ **Pick the person you feel closest to and most open with.** Spend a few minutes every day just listening to what this person is saying. Give them feedback: what they said and how you think they felt. Avoid making judgments or giving advice. Check to see if what you heard was what they meant.

○ **After watching a movie have a discussion with family or friends about how the characters felt and why they felt that way.**

Notes

1. Steven J. Stein, Ph.D., and Howard E. Book, M.D., *The EQ Edge: Emotional Intelligence and Your Success* (Mississauga, ON: John Wiley & Sons Canada, Ltd., 2006), p. 126.
2. Lorraine Grubbs-West, *Lessons In Loyalty: How Southwest Airlines Does It—An Insider's View* (Dallas: CornerStone Leadership Institute, 2005), p. 85.

CHAPTER 11

Healthy Relationships

"Love thy neighbor as thyself,
but choose thy neighborhood."

—AUTHOR LOUISE BEAL

Even though we may think that winning millions of dollars in the lottery will make us happy, facts and research tell us quite a different story. All of the research that has been done tells us that money and material possessions, after a certain point, have little to do with the amount of happiness we experience in our lives. The kinds of relationships we are able to form with others, conversely, have been shown to have a strong impact on how happy we are. With all the evidence that suggests our emotional well-being revolves around the quality of relations we form with others, you would think that this would be a major focus in people's lives.

Unfortunately, many people continue to spend a major amount of time and energy accumulating material wealth, while giving relationship building the short shrift. They continue to wonder why they don't feel happy and fulfilled, even though they have been successful at gathering possessions they thought would bring them satisfaction and contentment. Someone told me the other day that it seems many people spend more time and effort in choosing a house, vehicle, or other major purchase than they do in selecting someone with whom they plan, at least at the time, to spend the rest of their lives.

Our relationships with others are capable of bringing out the extremes of our emotions, from the heights of ecstasy to the depths of despair. Although the work involved in finding, creating, and growing healthy relationships is immense, the rewards by far make the effort worthwhile. There are few truly happy hermits. Most of us crave intimate relationships with other people. *Intimate* in this case does not mean sexual. It means having the type of relationship with someone that involves trust, someone with whom we can be ourselves and openly share our dreams, hopes, fears, joys, and sorrows. It has been said that if you have one true friend in this life, you should consider yourself fortunate. According to Stephen Covey, we need to build trust in our relationships using an "emotional bank account." Every time we do something to strengthen our ties with someone, we deposit into that account. There are many ways to do this. Listening to the person, being there when she needs us, keeping secrets she tells us in confidence, and being supportive of her dreams and aspirations are all ways that we build up that account. Others include remembering things about the person, keeping commitments, respecting his judgments and opinions even if we do not agree with them, and showing a genuine interest in his life.

When our account is healthy, when we have built up a high level of trust, our relationship frees itself from the common bounds of casual interaction with others. Since our trust has been built up, we become honest and authentic in ways that might not be tolerated in less well-developed relationships. There will be a sense of security, knowing that the fabric of the relationship is strong and able to withstand disagreements, even heated ones. It is much easier to ask for forgiveness from a friend after a quarrel if you have established a track record with the person. Establishing mutually rewarding relationships requires courage, commitment, self-discipline, and empathy. The more important the relationship, the more time should be spent building up your emotional bank account.

One thing that really irritates me is when someone I consider a friend gets involved in a romantic situation and totally forgets the friends who were there before this relationship began. Then, when the relationship cools as quickly as it heated up, that person is calling you, wanting to spend time with you again. People who do this are dependent individuals, insecure in their own worth. In their desperation, they give themselves completely over to someone who has little or no emotional bank account with them and forget those who have built up their account. Quickly draining their account with these people, they are surprised to find that their actions are resented, and their account is in a negative balance when they attempt to reestablish their relationships.

When you begin a relationship, respect those who have positive balances in their accounts with you. Your friends, family, and even your dog have a proven track record that puts them before the new interest in your life. Give these people their due, and they will be there for you. Yes, building a relationship will take away from friends and other interests, but true friends will accept that and be happy for you. As the relationship moves on and the person's account grows, you will want to spend more time together. This will necessitate a shift in priorities and giving more time and effort to building the primary relationship. However, part of a strong primary relationship is respect, including respecting the right of your partner to maintain, to some degree, the friendships that have nourished them in the past.

Romance Is Not a Cure-All

In many cases, we can't resist the temptation of a romantic relationship as a solution to our feelings of emptiness. Even though deep down we often know better, we opt for the quick fix, the easy solution, and the one that offers some immediate gratification. There is allure, excitement, and hope (which we later realize is false) attached to the situation. The pain comes afterward. The temptation of having others fill our needs is much more alluring than the idea of doing our own inner work. Working on ourselves seems to be tiresome, hard work by comparison. We sometimes do not see immediate results and the process is a long and arduous one. Unfortunately, we usually have to reach a place where we can no longer tolerate the pain of failed relationships before we are ready to begin our journey toward building a better self.

Begin with Yourself

The starting point for developing all relationships is the relationship we have with ourselves. It is, so to speak, the mother of all relationships. Unless we have done the work necessary to make our inner landscape a good place to be, we have no chance of developing an outer world that is healthy. All the emotional work that we need to do will not be effective if we are unable to properly manage our own emotions. Before we can become interdependent, we must first become independent. Some people go looking for others to fill the space within themselves that is missing. This simply doesn't work. In relationships, two halves do not make a whole. Only two whole, well-functioning people can create a healthy relationship. Sure, it may go well through some sunny times, but when difficulties arise, as they will in any relationship, things will not work out.

Healthy Relationships at Work

Building solid relationships with others is as important for success in the workplace as it is in our personal lives. In the last few years, the corporate world has shown an increased interest in, and respect for, the so-called soft skills, or people skills. Studies have consistently shown that the ability to get along with people is the most important aspect of how successful we will be at work, even more so than technical skills. Most jobs require teamwork and the need to work together at some level. There are few jobs that are so narrow and technical that people skills are not necessary to be successful in them. Even in occupations that we consider to be highly technical in nature, such as engineering, employees who get promoted are usually those who demonstrate an ability to work well with others.

In the last several years, workplace leadership programs have increasingly been using emotional intelligence theories and training to develop and improve people skills in their present and future leaders. As one consultant put it so elegantly, "There is no shortage of managers, but there is a crucial shortage of leaders." Although good interpersonal skills are essential for employees at all levels of an organization, they are crucial for good leaders.

Positive Leadership

In his book *Working with Emotional Intelligence*, Daniel Goleman looks at a study conducted by the U.S. Navy on the styles of the commanding officers.

> The superior leaders managed to balance a people-oriented personal style with a decisive command role. They did not hesitate to take charge, to be purposeful, assertive, and businesslike. But the greatest difference between average and superior leaders was in their emotional style. The most effective leaders were more positive and outgoing, more emotionally expressive and dramatic, warmer and more sociable (including smiling more), friendlier and more democratic, more cooperative, more likeable and "fun to be with," more appreciative and trustful, and even gentler than those who were merely average.[1]

When employee satisfaction levels within organizations have been studied, dissatisfaction with leadership has come out as the most common reason for leaving the workplace. Leaders have a tremendous ability to impact the staff under them in both positive and negative ways. Effective leaders are able to use their people skills to encourage, motivate, and get the most from their employees, while ineffective ones can cause morale and productivity to plummet. Realizing that this affects the bottom line, organizations are putting more emphasis on developing effective people skills at all levels of leadership.

Customer Service

Southwest Airlines has a long history of developing strong emotional connections among their staff, the organization, and their customers. Stories abound about staff going far above and beyond to help out customers. In one case, an employee took a stranded female customer to his sister's place to spend the night. There was another example of an elderly man, recently released from the hospital, who had been dropped off by his sister-in-law to catch a flight to see his family on Christmas Eve. Since that flight was canceled, staff got him a hotel room and transportation at the company's expense. By ensuring that he caught the first available flight the next day, they showed the true spirit of Christmas. It is this kind of customer service that has earned Southwest Airlines a loyal customer following.

Robin Sharma, in *Greatness Guide Book 2* speaks about making emotional connections to customers. While many businesspeople think that they are fighting for a share of what their client spends, Sharma feels that what they are actually going after is a share of the client's emotional goodwill. Using examples from things he feels attached to, such as Colombian coffee and his well-used Levi jeans, he makes a compelling case that customers buy because they make an emotional connection to a product or organization. He argues that if companies can form this type of connection with customers, they will not be affected by competitors who offer better deals. Such companies, he claims will not only survive but thrive under all conditions.[2]

> "Make yourself necessary to somebody. Do not make life hard to any."
>
> —RALPH WALDO EMERSON,
> AMERICAN ESSAYIST, PHILOSOPHER, AND POET

Eric's Story

Eric and Brad were sitting in a local coffee shop playing chess one weekend afternoon. Both were in their early forties and had gone to school together. Academically both had excelled, coming out in the top 10 percent of their class. To someone without further background information, these were two old school buddies spending some time together. This picture would be totally inaccurate.

About the only thing that Brad is willing to do with Eric is play chess, and this he does only out of a sense of duty. Brad is not Eric's friend; in fact, Eric has no friends—only acquaintances who will tolerate him long enough to play a game of chess. The differences between Eric and Brad are like night and day, even though they both graduated from the same school with basically the same grades and potential. Eric has been living on government support programs and a small inheritance for the majority of his adult life. After leaving school he did find a few jobs, one that even lasted for several years. However, they were not jobs that required him to use his mental abilities.

The problem is that Eric has absolutely no people skills. He is narcissistic and believes that he is smarter than everyone else. Not one to keep his opinions to himself, he constantly tells others how they should live their lives. Even though he was technically competent in the jobs he had, he always felt that he was smarter than his supervisors and did not hesitate to tell them so. Obviously, this did not win him many friends among his superiors and coworkers, and he ended up getting fired from virtually every job that he had. While he was able to befriend people for a short period with his ability to impress them with his vast knowledge, they soon wanted nothing to do with him. When he saw them hanging around with other people, he made rude and sarcastic remarks to them, further alienating himself. Eric had virtually no interest in the lives of those around him and only talked about himself in conversation. Even when he attempted to give someone a compliment, he managed to turn it into an insulting remark. He would frequently say things like, "That's a nice shirt for a loser." Needless to say, this did not earn him too many friends.

Several years ago, after many years of unemployment, Eric got some training and was ready to begin a new career. He managed to get a job in another city. People who knew him made bets on how long it would be before he would be back. The person who bet two weeks won. The outcome was quite predictable. It was only a few days before Eric started telling his new boss how he should run his business. His boss did not appreciate the advice and within two weeks fired him.

Eric has little insight into his situation and does not see that he has a problem. It's everyone else who is "screwed up." Many who know Eric believe that he is suffering from a type of personality disorder. Although Eric's case is rather extreme, you likely know people similar to him.

Then Eric had an epiphany of a sort. He was at the funeral of a work colleague, Greg, from one of the first jobs that Eric had after he left school. While they were not friends in the typical sense, they had remained in touch and shared a common interest in complaining and putting others down. Eric was shocked to find so few people at Greg's funeral. In chatting briefly with another mourner, he found out that Greg was not well liked and had made few friends in his lifetime. How sad, thought Eric, when it suddenly occurred to him that he and Greg were similar in many ways. He had a vision of his own funeral, with few mourners, if he continued on with his life the way he was.

Initially, he became quite depressed and raged at all the people whom he saw as being too stupid to appreciate his insight and genius. He could not, however, keep his delusion up for too long before realizing that he needed to make some real changes in his life. Reluctantly, he came to the conclusion that he needed help. Like Ebenezer Scrooge's visions of Marley, visions of Greg's lonely funeral kept coming back to him. He became aware of a longing to have friends, like other people, to date once in a while, and even have a regular girlfriend.

One of the first things that Eric was able to change was to curb his impulsive tendencies to make cutting and sarcastic remarks to people whenever he disagreed with anything that they were saying. Over time, he noticed that while old acquaintances still remained aloof, it didn't seem that they were as anxious to get out of his presence. Giving compliments to others and being supportive is very difficult for Eric. It does not come naturally and he has had to make a concerted effort to look for nice things to say to people. At first, it was all he could do to avoid being nasty and negative. As he slowly breaks himself of this habit, he is finding it easier to focus on the positive.

One of the difficulties for Eric in finding employment was his tendency to be negative and sarcastic even during the interview. This virtually assured him that he would not be offered the job. At this point Eric has been employed for a full six months. Although this may not seem like a long time, for Eric it is a record and an indication that he has been able to curb his most self-destructive tendencies.

One day his boss came up to him and accused him of making a mistake. Since it was a coworker who was working during that time, and not Eric, the boss was making an obvious mistake. The old Eric would have blown up, called his boss derogatory names, and likely been fired. Instead, Eric, without any hostility or anger, calmly explained to his boss that he had not been working during that time. For Eric, this was a major step in his change process and he felt calm and confident for the rest of the week.

"Do not protect yourself by a fence, but rather by your friends."

—CZECH PROVERB

Techniques for Increasing Healthy Relationships

○ **Pick a person at work, a club, or a social environment whom you would like to know better.** Whenever you talk to this person, concentrate on remembering one or two things about the person's life that are important to him or her. Write them down shortly afterward if you have trouble remembering. When you see the person again, ask about these things.

○ **Remember important dates and events in the lives of people who matter to you, such as birthdays and anniversaries.** Write them in a book you keep for that purpose. If you don't see them on those occasions, send a card or call them.

○ **Ask people questions about themselves.** Don't worry about getting too personal (within reason, of course), as people love to talk about themselves.

○ **When talking to others, pay attention to the amount of time you talk and the amount of time you listen.** If you find yourself talking more than 50 percent of the time, make a conscious effort to curtail speaking and spend more time listening.

○ **Do random acts of kindness.** At the office, bring in treats unexpectedly and for no specific occasion. Give flowers to your partner, spouse, girlfriend, or boyfriend when there is no special occasion. Mark this in your calendar at work or home so you remember to do it until it becomes second nature.

○ **When someone close to you is experiencing a difficult time, due to the loss of a loved one or for any reason, call and offer to help.**

Notes

1. Daniel Goleman, *Working with Emotional Intelligence* (New York: Bantam Books, 1998), p. 188.
2. Robin Sharma, *Greatness Guide Book 2* (New York: HarperCollins, 2007), p. 132.

CHAPTER 12

Social Responsibility

"You are not here to make a living. You are here
to enable the world to live more amply, with greater vision,
and with a finer spirit of hope and achievement. You are
here to enrich the world. You impoverish
yourself if you forget this errand."

—FORMER U.S. PRESIDENT WOODROW WILSON

Can you imagine a world where everyone looked out only for his or her own self-interest? Try to envision a world in which nobody cared about anyone else. Quite frightening, isn't it? I find it hard to envision such a place. When I do, I imagine violent gangs, murdering anyone who stands in their way, or pirates, staying together only because as a group they are able to become richer faster than they could as individuals. Yet, even in these groups, I imagine there must be some form of caring for each other that goes beyond immediate gain.

I'm sure you are familiar with the saying by the seventeenth-century English author, John Donne: "No man is an island." It encompasses the essence of the concept of social responsibility. We are all on this earth together and our actions, or lack of them, impact a lot of people around us. We are socially responsible to the degree that we see ourselves as being part of something larger than ourselves. Socially responsible people have a sense of duty to make the world a better place in which to live.

The Importance of Community

Another mark of great organizations, Robin Sharma claims, is their ability to build structures that allow everyone to feel safe and be respected for their contributions and uniqueness. These organizations are able to tap into the most basic needs of fitting in to something greater than ourselves that are an intrinsic part of our human nature.[1]

Most of us likely do not feel that we have any direct impact on the world. After all, we are not world leaders, in whose hands the fate of millions of people lie. As Mother Teresa said, "We cannot do great things, we can only do small things in a great way." However, we do impact our own micro version of the world, our communities in which we live. By doing our part to improve our own environment, we contribute in some manner to making our own world better. The children's soccer coach who volunteers hours of his or her time encouraging and inspiring the players may never know the difference he or she has made in a young person's life. Think of the things you have done in your life that would not have been possible if someone had not been willing to donate their own time.

Wonderful organizations such as Girl Scouts, Boy Scouts, and Big Brothers are only a few of many that help to shape future generations. They are all dependent on people who are willing to contribute their time or resources to the overall good. On another level, social responsibility means respecting the rights of others, and obeying laws that were put into place to protect all of us. It means doing our piece to protect the environment. Even though it takes time and effort on our part, we usually receive no external benefit directly.

Whether it is through volunteering or paid work, it has been shown that work that helps others brings us satisfaction and happiness. Tom W. Smith, director of General Social Survey (GSS) at the National Opinion Research Center at the University of Chicago has found that the people who reported the highest level of happiness and satisfaction were those that had jobs serving other people. The benefits of helping others out are enormous. One of the best-known ways for people who are dealing with feelings of depression to help themselves is to help others. One therapist I know recommends to patients who are feeling down to find someone who feels worse than they do and help cheer up that person.

Because we tend to live out what we think about, if we are thinking thoughts of what we are lacking, then we will experience feelings of sadness. It can be difficult to change our thoughts from our focus on what we don't have to thoughts of gratitude. One way to do this is to find someone who needs help and help them. This will help take the focus off of ourselves and help us see that, regardless of our situation, there are always things that we can be grateful for. Helping does not have to involve people. If we are animal lovers, spending time with a homeless puppy can bring us feelings of satisfaction and happiness.

Although doing volunteer work has always been a part of my life, I was especially involved during a period of unemployment. It was a difficult time for me. Getting out and helping those less fortunate took my mind off my own problems and helped me to feel that I was contributing something worthwhile to society. While I am a strong advocate of volunteerism for everyone, I feel it is crucial for anyone who finds himself or herself involuntary unemployed.

Although there are numerous individuals who have dedicated their lives to serving others, Mother Teresa and Albert Schweitzer are probably two of the best-known examples. Mother Teresa dedicated her adult life to helping some of the most desperately poor on earth in the slums of Calcutta. Albert Schweitzer, a talented physician, chose to spend his life helping eradicate disease and illness in Africa and built a clinic that today continues the work he began.

Jimmy Carter, after losing the election to Ronald Reagan, went through a difficult transition period. No longer having a powerful position and being out of the limelight has always been a difficult situation to accept for those who once held responsible and high-profile positions, but Jimmy Carter found meaning in helping others. He became a spokesperson for Habitat for Humanity, a nonprofit organization that builds affordable housing for those who otherwise would not be able to afford to own their own homes. Not only did the Carters become one of Habitat for Humanity's most well-known benefactors, they regularly travel around the country and help out in the actual construction of the homes. The Carters are still very active and involved in their community.

Qualities of a Helper

People who score high in the social responsibility area also tend to be strong in empathy. They are sensitive to the needs of others and have a strong internal drive to contribute. As well, they tend to be grateful for what they have been given in life and want to share it. Generally, these people are happy and optimistic, insofar as they choose to think the best of others. Another common denominator of people who generously volunteer their time is that they have themselves been through some hardship or crisis.

Social responsibility is the easiest of all of the emotional intelligence traits on which to rate people, because it is visible and public. It is one of the traits where women tend to score higher overall. One of the explanations may be that throughout history the nurturing role of staying home and looking after the family has been bestowed on women. This role has increased women's nurturing capacity and leads them to become predominant in traditional care-giving roles such as nursing. Men, while not traditionally raised to show emotions or to be nurturing, are beginning to be more open to these areas. Organizations like the Mankind Project encourage men to express and share feelings, look after each other, and contribute to their communities.

While individuals who have unselfishly responded to community needs have always been the unsung heroes in our world, organizations are increasingly becoming involved in contributing to their communities. A large construction company has for the last couple of years paid the full salaries of tradespeople employed by them for working on a Habitat for Humanity project.

One of the benefits of helping others is that it increases our awareness of the things that we have in our lives that we can be grateful for. Dr. Michael McCullough at the University of Miami found that people with feelings of gratitude tended to have more vitality and optimism, suffered less stress, and had fewer episodes of clinical depression than the overall population. Dr. Robert Emmons of the University of California at Davis did a study on people who kept a journal in which they kept track of things to be grateful for. He found that this group enjoyed better health, were more optimistic, exercised more regularly, and felt they were happier than those that did not keep such journals.

> "We are prone to judge success by the index of our salaries or the size of our automobiles rather than by the quality of our service and relationship to mankind."
>
> —MARTIN LUTHER KING, JR.

The House That Love Built

Southwest Airlines exemplifies giving back to their communities through their involvement with Ronald McDonald Houses. Founded in 1984 in Philadelphia by Dr. Audrey Evans and Philadelphia Eagles' right end Fred Hill, whose daughter had leukemia, the houses offer accommodation, compassion, and support for families who have children in hospitals. The program has since expanded and Ronald McDonald House Charities provide an array of services to improve the health and well-being of children around the globe and has become one of the largest not-for-profit organizations in the world. At every location that Southwest serves, staff and their families spend countless hours visiting, cooking meals, and comforting the children and their parents. Starting in Houston, employees began the practice of cooking monthly dinners at the local Ronald McDonald House. This started a practice of employees cooking dinner during June and November of each year at all houses within the Southwest system. A particularly heartfelt story about the relationship between a little girl with leukemia and Southwest staff is told to us by Tonda Montague, director of employee relations.

> Due to my involvement with the Ronald McDonald House, I was one of the employees asked to be in the commercial Southwest was filming at the Fort Worth Ronald McDonald House. On that day, I met the person who taught me the most about life—the person who touched my heart and made me realize the greatest

joy one can experience is sharing with others and to get the most out of life each and every day because life can be so uncertain.

It still amazes me how much I learned from that vivacious five-year-old who bounced into my life that day. We became instant friends, and during the next three years we did indeed learn a lot from each other. One thing Shea taught me was to never feel sorrow—she was too spunky for that. With Shea, every day was a celebration of life.

I visited her often at M.D. Anderson Hospital, and through all that pain she always asked about her friends in Southwest. We celebrated her sixth, seventh, and eighth birthdays at the Houston Ronald McDonald House, and I will never forget the time we gave her family a $3,000 check of donations from Southwest employees and as they drove off, Shea yelled: "Thanks for the million dollars." Or the time she barreled over the table as the Houston mechanics presented her with a bicycle. She was so appreciative of all we did for her.

In my heart, I never believed she would leave us. And I guess she really hasn't, because I feel her presence each and every day.[2]

"The best way to cheer you up is to cheer someone else up."

—MARK TWAIN, AMERICAN HUMORIST,
SATIRIST, LECTURER, AND WRITER

Rachel and Ed's Story

Rachel and Ed's life was hectic. Between soccer practices and dance and music lessons for their children, they were on the go from early morning until late at night every day of the week. Despite their busy schedules, they still had time to reach out and extend themselves beyond their immediate family. When asked what possessed them to add further to their already active schedules, both agreed that they wanted their children to be able to appreciate what they had and develop a sense of sharing and caring about those less fortunate. Ed loved playing soccer and, while growing up, had been a star player in his school. Since he had two sons who were now playing soccer, he decided he would offer to coach one of their teams. Rachel, between taking the children to their various activities, managed to find time to deliver meals to shut-in seniors a couple of times a month.

As the children grew up and left home, Rachel and Ed continued to be heavily involved in charities. Because Ed's business had been quite successful, they did not have financial concerns. Through the various organizations in which they were involved, they started a process to collect school supplies and donations of clothing for children in third-world countries. Ed and Rachel made a number of trips to a selected Central American country and personally delivered the materials to the children in a school they had chosen. One of their fondest memories of these times was the smiles of joy on the children's faces when they unexpectedly received some bright article of clothing.

Ed's social responsibility did not stop at his personal life, however. His company contributed to the community in a large way. As a construction company with more than twenty employees, they were able to take the lead on constructing a Habitat for Humanities home every year. Each employee was given a day off per month with full pay to perform this community service. The company also donated a great deal of material and used their equipment for the projects. Ed encouraged the employees and their families to donate their own time as well and many of them did. Although his business was known for high turnover, the company was well known for having a core of long-term loyal employees and had a reputation in the community for being a great place to work.

Ed and his sons who were involved in the company came up with an informal way of interviewing potential employees. They would ask the person being interviewed to spend some time introducing themselves to the staff and chatting for a few minutes to find out about what they did. In the meantime, Ed and his sons would leave, telling the potential employee that they would be back in half an hour or so. Unbeknownst to the job seekers, the employees had been coached in different scenarios to simulate a working situation where they would be struggling to accomplish something on their own, something that would be easier to do if they had a helping hand.

Afterwards, the employees would report back to Ed and his sons about whether the job seeker had taken the initiative to offer a hand and how quickly the candidate reacted to the employee's need for help. For example, the electrician would be struggling and straining to get a heavy panel into place, a job that would be made much easier and quicker if he or she had an extra pair of hands. The job seekers who quickly took the initiative to offer the worker the needed help were the most likely to be hired. Scenarios were also set up whereby it looked as if someone had accidentally dropped or lost something. Seeing the article, would the job seeker pick it up and turn it in, or ignore it since it was not their responsibility and they were not directly affected. Although they might seem like small and insignificant events to us, to Ed and his family the reaction of the job seeker to these staged scenarios were indicators as to their degree of teamwork orientation and concern for others. Since actions speak louder than words, Ed and his family found that what people did when they had no expectations placed on them was a much more effective way to screen for good employees. Although there were other issues that came up with employees after they were hired, they almost always hired people who were hardworking, good team players, responsible, and gave back to the community.

Rachel passed away several years ago, after battling breast cancer for a number of years. Ed, still healthy and active, continues to do the work that was so much a part of their lives. He feels very fortunate that he is still able to contribute, as it helps him cope with his loss. It also gives him a purpose and meaning to his life. Recently he spent two months in Somalia helping in the construction of a school. Cameron, Ed's son, has taken over control of the family company, giving Ed more time to do the charity work that he finds so fulfilling. Cameron continues on in the tradition of service that was so important to his father. On occasion, when he finds time in his hectic schedule, he accompanies his father on foreign-aid missions. For Cameron, these are special bonding times that the two of them get to spend together. Ed is at a total loss to understand how healthy people at his age (he is now seventy-three) can stand to sit around and do little with their time but get older, when there is so much in the world that needs to be done.

Ed speaks with great pride of his children, telling everyone how well they are doing. Recently, he went to an award ceremony sponsored by the city in which they live. Sarah, their youngest daughter who works as a nurse, was being honored for her work with inner-city residents. It was a very special moment for Ed, one he wished Rachel had been alive to see.

"Do definite good, first of all to yourself, then to definite persons."

—JOHN LANCASTER SPALDING, ROMAN CATHOLIC BISHOP

Techniques for Increasing Social Responsibility

- Set a certain amount of time aside that you will give regularly toward a worthwhile cause that you choose. Decide how much time you can donate and guard that time by giving it the same importance as exercise and recreational time.

- Choose a worthy cause. Make it something you have a personal connection with. If you have lost a loved one to cancer, for example, volunteer at the Cancer Society. The personal connection will give you a better sense that you are contributing your time to something worthwhile.

○ Become more active in your workplace, church, or other organization you belong to by looking for opportunities to take on extra responsibility.

○ Next time you see someone on the road with a stalled vehicle, and it is safe to do so, stop and offer to help.

○ If you see someone at work or at home struggling with their workload, and you have some spare time, ask if you can help them.

○ Think of the talents that you have and the gifts that have been bestowed on you. Consider ways that you can share these gifts with others through charitable acts.

Notes

1. Robin Sharma, *Greatness Guide Book 2* (New York: HarperCollins, 2007), p. 166.
2. Kevin and Jackie Freiberg, *NUTS! Southwest Airlines' Crazy Recipe for Business and Personal Success* (New York: Broadway Books, 1998), p. 241.

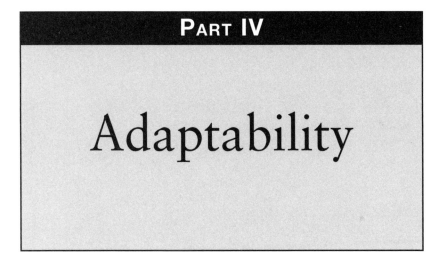

PART IV

Adaptability

CHAPTER 13

Problem Solving

"Men solve far more problems by hate, love, lust, rage,
sorrow, joy, hope, fear, illusion, or some other inward
emotion, than by reality, authority, any legal standard,
judicial precedent, or statute."

—Roman Statesman and Philosopher Cicero
(106 bc–43 bc)

Confidence in our abilities and being able to overcome and deal with our fears are important aspects in how well we are able to come up with solutions to the problems we face. Generally, people consider problem solving to be something we use our intellectual thinking ability for. But emotions play a role that is just as important, and that can also be extremely informative.

When Others Are Involved

Since many of our problems involve others, our ability to deal with people is critical to how well we are able to solve problems. Because most problem solving involves some interaction, our success will be determined by how effectively we are able to get the help we need.

The basis of this is quite simple. Remember the last time that you went out of your way to help someone? Was the person you helped someone you liked or was it someone whom you couldn't stand? Chances are you liked the person, otherwise you would not have chosen to help him or her. Of course, there are many situations in which we help others to solve problems regardless of how we feel about them, such as in our workplace in order to keep our jobs. Even when required, however, we can choose whether the person will receive our full effort or absolute minimum. The person who will receive our full effort will be the one who has been able to form a close positive relationship with us. I can think of few problems where we are an island unto ourselves, most problems require the involvement of others to some degree to solve effectively. The relationship that has been formed between the person asking for help and the person receiving it determines whether the receiver will get the minimum or full effort.

Studies have shown that the more we need to interact with others in order to problem solve, the more critical our EI skills become. Some people assume that occupations that are highly technical in nature are big on cognitive skills and don't require much in terms of people skills. It was found in the computer sciences that the programmers and other technicians whose main interactions are problem solving with machines required fewer EI skills than those who had to work in a team unit. But regardless of the technical nature of the occupation, advancement in the field requires an increasing interdependence on others. This is where strong EI skills or lack of them will factor in to how successful a person becomes in that organization. EI skills in problem solving are just as important to technicians when they are self-employed as when they are employed in an organization and attempting to work their way up.

Several years ago, I had purchased some revenue property and was in need of an electrician. I ended up choosing Ken, a self-employed tradesman who was friendly, had great people skills, and took the time to explain the work that needed to be done in plain terms that I easily understood. Of course, I believed that he was also quite competent, but it was not his technical skill that got him the work, but his EI attributes. I felt that most of the electricians whom I had used were competent. However, they did not have Ken's level of people skills.

Asking for help and getting others to want to help us are skills involving our own emotions and an awareness of other people's emotions. There is a balance between doing for ourselves and asking for help from others. Ideally, the healthiest balance is for us to do as much as we can for ourselves, but to be comfortable asking for help when we truly need it. Many people have difficulty in both of these areas, but with practice we can improve.

Thinking—and Feeling—Our Way to the Solution

EI can help us take advantage of our thinking skills, or lack of EI could keep us from using them to their best advantage. One of the questions that I come across when speaking is, "If a person has good EI, can they do well if they aren't very smart"? The answer is yes; people who have good EI can do well even if they do not have high cognitive (IQ) intelligence. The ideal situation would be someone who has a great deal of both types of intelligence. Earlier in the book, I mentioned a number of people who had very high IQs, such as Ted Bundy, but had a great deal of trouble functioning in society. The trial judge in his case, in which Bundy defended himself, remarked how good a job Bundy was doing defending himself, and how, under different circumstances he would welcome having Bundy present a case in front of him. If Bundy would have had EQ to match his high IQ, his potential to achieve things in his life would have been great. As it was, Bundy's lack of EI severely hampered his ability to use his high IQ for his own benefit and the benefit of society.

Just as emotions can hamper us, so they can help us. Emotions are the best way to do a pre-check on the decisions we are about to make. If we feel good about what we are to do, even though it may be the more difficult decision to make, we are making the right decision. We are unable to monitor our thoughts constantly since experts tell us that the average person has 60,000 thoughts per day. Our emotions are an excellent way of aligning ourselves with thoughts that are in our best self-interest. If we are feeling good, we are thinking positive uplifting thoughts that will benefit and sustain us in life.

Benefits of Good Problem-Solving Skills

"Difficulties are opportunities to better things; they are stepping-stones to greater experience. . . . When one door closes, another always opens; as a natural law it has to, to balance."

—Author Brian Adams

By doing as much as we can for ourselves, we enhance our independence and develop good self-regard. Developing our ability to cope with and overcome problems also has a positive effect on our ability to tolerate stress. Every problem that we successfully solve gives us increased confidence that we will be able to solve the next one. People who become stressed at the prospect of facing problems have a tendency to avoid problems. In doing so, they will miss out on opportunities because reaching goals in life involves facing and solving problems that come up along the way. Instead of trying to avoid problems, we are better off becoming better problem solvers.

"Problems are only opportunities in work clothes."

—Henri Kaiser, American Industrialist

"Some people think only intellect counts: knowing how to solve problems, knowing how to get by, knowing how to identify an advantage and seize it. But the function of intellect is insufficient without courage, love, friendship, compassion and empathy."

—Author Dean Koontz

David's Story

Problem solving has been a big part of David's working life for more than thirty years. For a large portion of that time, he worked as a dispatcher for a number of bus and trucking firms. Many years ago, David had been attending university and was looking for a summer job. When he saw the posting in the Student Services area for drivers and tour guides in Alaska for the summer, he jumped at the opportunity. Spending the summer traveling around Alaska sounded to him like the dream summer job. While other students were working at minimum-wage menial jobs, he was experiencing the last frontier firsthand while meeting interesting people from all over the world.

One of the things the job frequently entailed was driving long distances alone to pick up a group. On one occasion, he had to travel from Whitehorse in the Yukon to Anchorage, Alaska, a distance of hundreds of miles, many of them through twisty mountain roads. To keep him company he asked a female traveler, whom he had met in Whitehorse, to accompany him on this long trip. About 200 miles from Anchorage, he had a mechanical breakdown. The throttle cable that ran from the engine at the back of the coach to the controls in front broke. David and his passenger were stranded in the middle of Alaska in the era before cell phones. When he walked to the nearest home and called the shop owned by his company to ask what to do, he was in for a rude awakening. The shop manager, whom he expected would help him out of his predicament, simply told him that he couldn't do anything for him. He said that he didn't know anyone in Anchorage to call for help, and that it happened too far from home base to be able to send out assistance.

David was shocked. His first impulse was to walk away from the broken motor coach, get a ride to Anchorage, and fly back home to California. He had never felt so alone and unsupported. Being raised to be responsible, however, David knew that he couldn't just leave. Working to overcome feelings of fear and anger, he considered his situation. Could he make temporary repairs with the material that was available, which would allow him to limp a disabled motor coach 200 miles through a mountain pass? The first experiment ended in failure. He propped open the throttle at the rear using a lock that he carried. However, the brakes soon began to get hot and started to smoke. This obviously wouldn't work, and could only cause further problems.

After a couple of hours pondering the problem from a number of alternatives, he saw a possible solution. There was an opening from inside the coach down to the engine compartment in the rear. If he could find a rope long enough, he could tie it to the throttle, run it along the inside of the motor coach, and control it from the front. A small gas station store down the road a couple of miles had a clothesline that was long enough. Making it work, though, would require teamwork. David's hands were occupied with steering and shifting gears on the coach. His traveling companion, Susan, would have to control the speed by alternately pulling and releasing the clothesline.

There were issues other than technical ones that came into play as well. David, considerably stressed by the thought of what lay ahead, also had to reassure Susan—who had doubts about her ability to carry out what she was being asked to do. At first, they were out of sync, with Susan pulling on the clothesline when David was trying to slow down or vice versa. After an hour or so, she was able to synchronize her role with David's shifting and the terrain of the highway. Exhaust fumes from the engine coming through the opening in the floor concerned Susan a great deal. Having made it through the mountain pass, with only 20 more miles of relatively flat road to go before Anchorage, she decided that the fumes were too much of a health hazard and she would be better off hitchhiking. Tired from the ordeal, David calmly listened to her concerns and tried to reassure her that with the windows open there was no danger of them suffering from carbon monoxide poisoning. After a long talk, she reluctantly agreed to get back into the bus and they made it to Anchorage. As they parted in Anchorage, David let Susan know how much he appreciated her determination, courage, and resilience. Without her, he would not have been able to make it.

David's manager, upon hearing about the trip back, was very impressed. For the rest of the season, David was rewarded by being given lucrative tours that had usually been awarded to senior drivers, not rookies like him. The story of David's trip was told to every new training class for years afterward.

Anticipating the possibility of road failures, David formed strategic relationships with people in many different states who could help him. He saw building these relationships and maintaining them as a vital part of his job and the business in which he worked. On many occasions, they paid off in that he was able to get help out to a stranded vehicle at all hours, after repair facilities were closed and it was hard to get help. It was a reciprocal relationship. The same people David could count on coming through for him knew they could also count on him to do whatever he could for them, should they require his assistance if they ran into a problem in his area. "Getting people to want to help you is not rocket science," David explains. "Think about the people in your life that you helped and wanted to help. Do you like those people? Have you helped people you don't like, unless it's a relative or someone you really have to help? Really, all it amounts to is that to get people to want to help you, the first thing to do is get them to like you," David expounded. Although his theory sounds simple, most basic truths are.

"A positive attitude may not solve all your problems, but it will annoy enough people to make it worth the effort."

—AUTHOR HERM ALBRIGHT (1876–1944)

Techniques for Problem Solving

- **Think of as many solutions as you can to every problem you encounter.** Get feedback from others with different viewpoints or perspectives to get a broader range from which to choose a solution.

- **Ask others for ideas and solutions.**

- **Practice anticipating and solving problems before they arise.** For example, what are some problems that could arise in everyday life? For example, your car could break down on the way to work. Think of what you would do if that happened. How many different solutions can you come up with? What is the best one? The one you would likely choose? Having done this exercise, what could you do now to make you better prepared in the event that it happened? I have done this exercise and have a list of phone numbers in my wallet—in the order that I would call. This actually came to be as my car did end up breaking down on the way to work several months ago. Having worked through this scenario and being prepared made the actual experience much less stressful for me.

- **Every day, come up with a number of solutions to an imaginary problem.** For example, your regular route to work is closed; your boss suddenly quits and leaves you all his work; or you spill something on your pants on the way to an important speech you have to make.

- **Play games with your children, spouse, or coworkers where you come up with a problem and try to identify as many different solutions as possible.**

- **Always think of problems as having more than one solution.** The more tools we have at our disposal, the better problem solvers we will become. Think in terms of better answers instead of right or wrong. The more solutions we have, the better our chances to pick a good solution. This works up to a point. Too many choices on the other hand can overwhelm and confuse us.

o **Take your ego out of the problem.** If someone has a better solution than you do, use it. Successful people have an array of tools with which to solve problems, theirs as well as those they borrow from others. They have learned to put their egos aside and use whatever information and ideas that work best. The mark of great leaders, such as John F. Kennedy, is that they are known for being able to admit when they are wrong.

o **Get away from needing to be right.** Instead, focus on becoming successful. Bill Gates, who is one of the world's wealthiest men, is willing to admit when he is wrong. Initially, he did not see the potential of the Internet. When he began to see that he had been mistaken, he immediately turned his belief system around and started to invest heavily in the Internet.

o **Reward yourself whenever you come up with a great solution to a problem.** It will give you added incentive for coming up with one for the next problem you face.

CHAPTER 14

Reality Testing

"Reality is merely an illusion,
albeit a very persistent one."

—Albert Einstein

How well we function in this world has a great deal to do with how accurately we view it. Although we all may think that we view things objectively, this is only an illusion. All of our perceptions and judgments are clouded by our past experiences and how we have chosen to view these experiences. Having said that, however, it is important that we make every effort to see the world as honestly as we can. If we are unable to see things as they really are, we may be missing opportunities that arise. Having realistic views of the world will also help us to avoid making poor decisions. Our decisions should, as much as possible, be made on evidence and fact, rather than on flights of fancy or wishful thinking.

Other Points of View

One of the best ways to stay close to reality is to consider information from as many sources as possible. For example, I always read columnists stating political viewpoints that are opposite from mine. Although I seldom agree with their ideas, it is important to consider the reasoning behind these views. At the same time, reading criticisms of views that

I hold dear challenges me to constantly rethink the basis for my own beliefs and judgments. Having changed my political stance in the past when I could no longer justify it, I like to think that I would be capable of changing again, if I discovered that there were other political beliefs that made more sense. It is always easier to let others do our thinking for us, and many people have resigned themselves to living this way. There are always family members, friends, politicians, religious leaders, managers, or coworkers who will be more than happy to tell us how we should lead our lives. It is easier for us to let someone else tell us how to live, thereby avoiding the responsibility that comes along with making our own choices. The price we pay for this decision is to give up control of our lives to others.

The Urge to Escape from Reality

Humanity has devised an unlimited means for avoiding and escaping from reality. I was reading an article on retirement in a leading financial publication the other day that stated a surprisingly large number of people, when questioned about their retirement plans, responded that winning a lottery played a major role. This is truly frightening, as reality will eventually burst their bubble. Addictions, whether to drugs, alcohol, video games, television, or even shopping, are often attempts to escape a reality with which we are unable or unwilling to deal. Some addictions, such as fitness, can be seen as being a positive thing, when they increase our feelings of well-being and enjoyment from life. An obsession with fitness can become unhealthy, however, if it is used to escape the reality that our body is aging.

Although reality is no doubt unpleasant for many people, escaping from it is not the answer. There are times when reality is so horrible that for psychological reasons we have to escape it temporarily to preserve our sanity. When my mother was dying of cancer in the hospital, we were able, for the most part, to talk openly about it. There were times, however, that she did not want to face reality at that point and told me so. This is a healthy coping mechanism. It would have been quite a different situation if we had both gone along acting like nothing was

119

wrong and talking about her going home in a short time. This would have cheated us both out of the opportunity to clear up any unfinished business and to say good-bye.

Styles of Dealing with Reality

There are two ways that people choose to deal with reality. In the first group are people who tend to see everything in the negative. They are the gloom-and-doom prophets, commonly known as pessimists. They have learned to see everything that they experience in the worst possible light. We all know people like this and probably avoid them like the plague. Motivational speakers tell us to run, don't walk, away from negative people, as they will bring us down. If a group of people has one negative person in it, that person can bring down the energy of the entire group. This is the group that will miss out on opportunities because they will simply not be able to see them, busy as they are focusing on the problems. Avoidance becomes their coping mechanism. They become rigid and inflexible, hoping that nothing changes since to them all change is bad.

On the other hand, there are people who tend to see everything in a positive light. These are the optimists. It is not that optimists do not see the downside of life; it's simply that they choose to focus on the positive. The group that it is dangerous to belong to is the group that chooses not to see the negative. Often referred to as Pollyannas, these people tend to sanitize and make good everything that they experience. Others tend to avoid individuals like this, not because they drain energy and bring them down, but because they can be so irritating in their denial. Unlike their opposites, the pessimists who dread change, this group is very upbeat about it, as they are toward everything else. Unable or unwilling to see real dangers, they often make bad decisions. These are the people, the walking victims, who are so often taken advantage of by the less scrupulous in our society.

The healthy road is not to ignore the dark side of human nature, but also not to live our lives focused on it. Whenever possible, it is healthier and more fulfilling to focus on the bright side.

"Reality is that which, when you stop believing it, doesn't go away."

—Author Philip K. Dick

Jody's Story

Lisa and Jody met while attending a support group for abused women. The two women started to go for coffee after their group on Wednesday nights. Jody was still with John, her husband of twenty years. When they had decided to get married, instead of looking for love, happiness, and all the other good stuff we are told to expect that a life shared with another person should bring, Jody made her marriage decision based on avoiding loneliness and the fear of becoming an old maid.

The abuse started within six months of their wedding. John regularly called her stupid, and started to put her and her family down. On occasion, when he got overly agitated, he would push or punch her. They did very little together and seldom went out. Claiming he was away on business, John often stayed away for a week at a time, seldom calling his wife while away. One time she called him at the hotel where he told her he was staying while on a convention for work. The desk clerk told Jody that her husband was not a registered guest there and there was no convention going on for his company. When she confronted him, he told her that it was a different hotel, but he had forgotten the name. When she told the story to her friends, it was obvious to them that her husband was having an affair. Jody, however, continued to be in denial, making up excuses for John. At one point, all of Jody's friends and family could see that the relationship was dysfunctional and unhealthy and advised her to leave. Even though she had offers of support from a number of friends, even offering her a temporary place to stay if she left, she chose to ignore the reality that her friends and family clearly saw. Her fear of being on her own kept her in stuck in an unhappy and dysfunctional relationship.

During their relationship her life was on hold. She stayed in her dead-end job and maintained contact with a few of her friends from college days, but did nothing to expand her range of friends or interests. One of her friends noticed that she still wore some clothes that she had worn at college. The friend thought that Jody was depressed and asked her to go for counseling. Jody shrugged off the suggestion, saying that there wasn't much a counselor could do. When her friend, who was enjoying her single life for the time being, was telling Jody about how happy she was in her life, Jody, looking downcast, blurted out, "At least I'm married." How sad, thought her friend, seeing it as an indicator of how hopeless and desperate Jody's life had become.

Although Lisa's husband never physically hit her, he had smashed dinner plates by throwing them against the kitchen wall. She had heard that violence against objects often leads to violence against people, and she was afraid that she would be the next target of his rage. Her brother, friends, and even her mother urged her to leave. After fourteen years of marriage, while her husband was out of town on business for a couple of days, she called in movers, packed up all her belongings, and left for good.

In two years' time, Lisa's life went from coping with the breakup to beginning to thrive. When she first joined the support group, she was hurting badly and needed their encouragement. Feeling much stronger and confident in herself now, she stayed in the group mainly to be supportive to newer members like Jody. Having received so much from the group in her time of great need, she felt the need to give something back.

When Lisa and Jody initially started getting together after their group, Lisa did a lot of listening and was very supportive. She empathized with Jody's situation as only someone who has also been there was able to. After several months, Lisa noticed that Jody had never mentioned any plans for leaving the relationship. When Jody had asked her husband to go for couple's counseling, he adamantly refused, telling her that their problems were all her fault and she was damn lucky that she had found someone like him, who would put up with her crap. He did not know that Jody was going to the group, because she lied and told him that her schedule had changed and she had to work late on Wednesdays. She was afraid that he would be furious if he found out.

It was obvious to Lisa, as well as to many of the other group members, that leaving was the only option. They were hoping Jody would come to the decision herself, and they would jump in and support her wholeheartedly. It became increasingly frustrating for them that this did not seem to be happening. Week after week it was the same complaints, but no plan of action as to what she was going to do about it.

Finally, over coffee one evening, Lisa asked Jody when she was planning to leave. Jody sidestepped the question, and for the rest of the night eased up on her complaints about how terrible things were living with John. Lisa continued to press Jody on her plans to get out of the nightmare that she was living. Several other members of the group were becoming tired of listening to Jody complain about her life with John week after week, but choosing not to do anything about it. A couple of them confronted her directly, telling her that they would be there for her if she left the jerk, but they did not wish to waste their time listening to her if all she wanted to do was continue to whine. At this point she began crying, which she usually did when she was told something she didn't want to hear.

Lisa, seeing Jody trapped in a bad relationship that was ruining her life, continued to bring up the topic of leaving John. At one point Jody became angry, accusing Lisa of being jealous of her because she was married and Lisa was not. Lisa was stunned, totally failing to understand how Jody could see anything positive in this marriage. She made up her mind that until Jody could face up to reality, all she was doing was enabling her to maintain a very dysfunctional and destructive relationship. At this point, she told Jody that when she made up her mind to get out of the relationship, she would be there for her. Until then, she did not wish to continue their friendship.

Since Jody had alienated her friends with her constant complaining at both work and in the group, she found herself without support to make any changes. She felt trapped in a rut and was completely unaware of how she had reached that point.

Techniques for Reality Testing

- Always look for as many sources of information and opinion as possible before developing a view on important matters.

- Seek out ideas and views that differ from yours. Ask yourself why these people believe that they are right. What evidence do they have?

- Check out as many people as possible to see if they see things as you do.

- Make a point of sounding out your ideas with people who think differently from you.

- Practice trying to see things from as many different perspectives as possible. One way is to have debates with your family and friends about various issues. Take the opposite side of an issue and defend it from that viewpoint.

- When you feel you have done a thorough job of investigating an issue or situation, make up your own mind.

- If you receive feedback from many different sources that the way you see things has flaws, be prepared to reconsider your beliefs.

CHAPTER 15

Flexibility

"If we don't change, we don't grow. If we don't grow,
we aren't really living."

—Author Gail Sheehy

The rate of change in our world is constantly increasing. Some social
scientists have been wondering lately if there is a limit to people's
capacity to change, and if there is, whether or not we are reaching that
limit. For some of us this change offers unlimited opportunity, and we
welcome it into our lives.

We tend to embrace change if we feel in control of the pace of change
and are certain that we will receive a benefit from it. Many people buy
lottery tickets, thinking that they would embrace the change that would
come with suddenly becoming wealthy and having more choices in their
lives. They foresee all the things that they would do if they could quit
their jobs and follow their dreams. They foresee that they would be in
control of the change and that the change would be positive.

The reality, however, is that most people are unprepared for the
change that will be thrust on them when they suddenly come into a
great deal of money because they cannot change who they are. Most
lottery winners come from working-class backgrounds. Should they
buy a large house in a new neighborhood full of wealthy people, they
discover that they have nothing in common with their new neighbors.

Accustomed to traveling on a budget, they find that they are rubbing elbows with unfamiliar moneyed classes whenever they travel in the luxury style. If they stay in their old jobs, they are often derided by coworkers for continuing to work and expected to buy lunch. They face a great deal of pressure over managing their newfound wealth. It is little wonder that many lottery winners end up saying that they wish it had never happened.

Others, however, dread change and wish we could slow the pace or stop change altogether. Typically people resist, deny, and avoid change if they only see that it will have negative consequences in their lives. Economic turndown, war, and natural catastrophes are changes that are dreaded by most people. Regardless, it is unlikely that the pace of change will slow. Today, more than at any other time in history, success is determined by our ability to be flexible. We are constantly forced to make changes to accommodate unforeseen circumstances and situations. People who embrace change are always looking for the positive that comes with it. While not ignoring the negative aspects, they choose to focus on the positive. As the Chinese philosopher said after his house burned down: "Now I can see the stars."

Think of the following race car driver analogy. The driver, representing emotional intelligence, has to continuously adapt to an environment that is changing by the minute, even by the second. Other cars are constantly veering in and out of his path. The road continually changes—one minute it is flat, and the next it curves. At any time, there is the possibility that the car may go into a skid, requiring immediate action. Another car may crash and become an obstacle. In some situations, the driver has a great deal of control, while in others very little. Regardless of the amount of control, flexibility allows the driver to get the most out of any given situation.

Robert Sternberg, a Yale Scholar and one of the world's leading authorities on intelligence, had this to say about the relationship of flexibility to success:

Not only does what is required for success differ in different fields and domains, it also differs over the course of one's career.

The characteristics that lead to success in entry-level management jobs, for example, are quite different from those that lead to success at the higher levels of management. At the lower levels, one largely follows; at the higher levels, one largely leads. At the lower levels, one may have little work to delegate; at the upper levels, one may have to delegate almost everything.[1]

Successful intelligent people are flexible in adapting to the roles they need to fulfill. They recognize that they will have to change the way they work to fit the task and situation at hand, and then they analyze what will have to be done and make it happen.

Qualities That Come with Flexibility

Success depends on our ability to react quickly and appropriately to new situations. Flexibility is related to a number of other emotional intelligence factors such as stress tolerance, independence, and self-regard.

Confidence

Feeling confident in ourselves directly impacts our feelings of how well we can adapt and successfully change. How successfully we feel that we have been able to deal with change in the past determines the level of confidence we will have when dealing with new changes.

Stress Management

It also requires that we be able to keep our stress at manageable levels. High levels of stress will make us less able to cope with change. A person who is unable to cope with a lot of stress will be easily overwhelmed by change. It is not that those who manage to adjust well to new situations do not feel stress; they have just found ways to not let stress levels get to the point where it impairs their ability to choose, make decisions, and act when appropriate. Again, having successfully dealt with changes in the past will reduce our anxiety level about change that we will encounter.

Independence

People with low levels of independence might view themselves as victims of change, feeling there is little they can do about it. More independent types will look at change differently by focusing on ways that they can use the change to benefit themselves. They may also feel more in control by not accepting change wholesale, but rather adopting aspects of change that they find beneficial and rejecting other areas that they find detrimental.

Feeling in Control

Having some sense that we are in the driver's seat of our lives is also a necessary precursor to flexibility. Feeling weak and out of control only increases our stress and desire to avoid involvement with anything new.

Embracing the Future

In most sports, successful athletes are those individuals who are the most flexible. A good example of a highly flexible athlete is hockey superstar Wayne Gretzky. Able to score from a multitude of situations, he had the knack of being able to predict where the puck would be several plays ahead, and get into the best possible scoring position. His high degree of flexibility allowed him to adapt quickly to take maximum advantage of every situation.

The future will belong to those who are able to adapt. Those unwilling to change will lose out. There is a saying to the effect that "if you are standing still, you are falling behind." Everything is constantly changing: technology, the economy, the environment, and the people around us. If we resist change or do not keep up, then the world and the people around us will leave us behind. In many cases, relationships end because one person changes and the other does not. Sometimes both people change and find out that the new person that they are with is not the one they knew back when they first met.

The way we view change has a lot to do with how successful we are at adapting to change. The creative types that look for all the wonderful things that change can bring to our lives welcome change. Creative, flexible people are those who love to learn and see excitement and adventure in exploring and learning new ways of doing things.

Those who are trapped in their old habits often have doubts and reservations about their ability to learn. They are pessimists who see change as imposing new demands on their set, clearly defined world.

Yet, the only thing that separates the creative optimist who loves to learn new things from the pessimist who dreads change is how they see change. If the pessimists only looked for things they have successfully adapted to and that have benefited their lives over the last few years, they would find lots of examples. Banking machines, cell phones, and the Internet have all made our lives much more convenient. Most people use these relatively new innovations quite effortlessly and with little thought. When they were first introduced, however, large numbers of people experienced anxiety about their ability to learn to use these new technologies, fearing that they would be left behind. We need to remember that it would simply not make economic sense for any company to develop a new consumer product that was beyond most people's ability to learn to use rather easily. The product would fail rather quickly. As well, political leaders who try to introduce ideas that the populace is not ready for doom themselves to political suicide. It is therefore ultimately in our hands as to how much change we are ready for and willing to accept.

Enhancing Our Flexibility

The great news is that all of us can become more flexible. Like other aspects of emotional intelligence, flexibility is learned. Try something new tomorrow. Start with something that is not that difficult for you and doesn't cause too much stress. Regardless of the outcome, look only for the positive. One thing positive is certain; you have learned something from the experience that is, in and of itself, positive. Even if it is only in a minor way, you will have expanded your world. If you are unable to see anything positive in the experience, ask someone you have confidence in to look for something positive. Think about the positive aspect they are seeing and incorporate it into your own thinking. Begin to make it a habit to begin to look at all new experiences in this way. As well, make it a habit to reward yourself for learning something new or adapting success-fully to a new circumstance. Don't compare yourself to others, because you will always find people who are more and less flexible. Simply focus on the things that you can be successful at.

Flexibility and Age

Many people have the misconception that we naturally become less flex-ible and stuck in our ways when we get older. This is simply not true. Show me an inflexible sixty-year-old and I'll show you someone who was inflexible at twenty. There are examples everywhere of highly flex-ible individuals who, well into their seventies and eighties, are taking on new challenges in their lives.

Several years ago Val, a friend of mine, retired from her job at age fifty-five. She purchased a small house in a fairly remote little town in the mountains, close to an area that she always enjoyed. She rented the house out and planned to do so until she moved there when she turned seventy. Until that time she was planning to, as she put it, "have adventures." She did just that, teaching English as a second language in various parts of the world, as well as traveling and living in areas that had always interested her. Taking up travel photography and writing travel articles, which she tried getting published in magazines, gave her constant challenges.

Making Mistakes

Flexibility and trying new ways of doing things naturally results in making mistakes. Organizations that want their staff to be flexible and creative have to let them know that making mistakes sometimes when one takes a risk is expected and acceptable. As long as the mistake resulted from an honest attempt to improve things, employees must be allowed to learn from their mistakes rather than be punished. There is no better way for an organization to show that honest mistakes are forgiven than by having management share stories of mistakes that they have made along the way. New hires will come to trust that if they try something new and it doesn't work out, it will not mean the end of the road in the organization.

Southwest Airlines believes that to get employees to be flexible and take risks they need to know that they will be treated with dignity and respect if they make a mistake. They believe that the cost of mistakes pales in comparison to the benefits of unleashing an employee's creativity and flexibility. Some of the company's most loyal and dedicated and enthusiastic employees have made significant mistakes in the past, and despite their errors, have gone on to bigger and better things in the organization. This willingness to forgive and forget has endeared and bonded these people to the organization. It has been described by some staff as an exercise in character building.

> " 'We must become the change we want to see'—Those are the words I live by."
>
> —MOHANDAS GANDHI

Kathryn's Story

Kathryn was part of the unit that made up a small division of a large corporation. The part of the company she worked for was a specialty unit. Their work was unique, although it complemented the overall business of the company. There were only ten members on staff, and they were somewhat isolated from the larger picture. This separation had both advantages and disadvantages. On the upside, they had more opportunities to be creative and try new ideas than did a larger office. Unfortunately, many of the staff members were not known to be overly flexible and open to new ideas.

Kathryn heard about emotional intelligence through a workshop she attended. When ideas for staff development were being bandied about during a unit meeting at work, she proposed that all of them take the emotional intelligence test. The results would be confidential, to be shared only between the test administrator and the individual staff members. In that way, everyone would have the opportunity to do some personal development work without anyone else knowing how they scored. All of the tests could then be added together to come up with a composite, or overall score for the unit. This score could be used to do some group work with their coworkers. The overall score would be confidential and it would not be possible to pick out anyone's individual score.

Some of the staff members were excited about the prospect, while others were hesitant, but all gave in to the urgings of the majority. Everyone, including the manager and supervisor, took the BarOn EQ-i and received feedback from a consultant who was brought in. Although their overall score was above average, flexibility was one of the areas in which the test indicated there was room for improvement. Kathryn was asked to come up with ongoing exercises they could do on a regular basis as a group to become more flexible.

One of the things that everyone agreed kept them from being more flexible was fear. In order to deal with fear, they looked at various possible scenarios and broke them down. For example, if we did this, what is the worst that could happen, what is most likely to happen, and what is the best that could happen? What was the likelihood that headquarters would shut them down? There was little evidence that this was likely to happen. If it did, most staff probably would be transferred to other areas rather than lose their jobs. On the contrary, they were able to come up with solid evidence that headquarters was pleased with the work they were doing and considered their unit, although small, to be an important component of their overall operation. In this way, staff were able to see that most of what they feared was not based on evidence and reality.

Through demystifying fear, it was felt that they would be able to remove one of the major barriers that kept them from trying new things. Staff members were all encouraged to use the same process individually to increase their own flexibility. A couple of the staff members were already highly flexible and prepared to assist their coworkers in becoming more open to change.

At first, it was difficult to see if there was any real change going on. The staff members who had adamantly opposed new ideas in the past were no longer openly expressing their opposition to ideas that were presented. This may have been due to not wanting to be identified as dinosaurs in the post–EI testing world more than their having embraced the notion that they needed to be more flexible. These individuals could still sabotage the process by subtly undermining it, or doing nothing to help.

After a year it was suggested that staff members switch jobs with each other for a period of time to gain a wider knowledge base and increase their skills. This was a radical idea for the organization and a year earlier would have been ridiculed immediately and dismissed. The usual people who were always opposed had reservations, but promised they would give the idea a try. It was agreed that if it didn't work out, they could always go back to their former positions. The best scenario was that they would come to enjoy the new challenge, and headquarters would see the unit as being dynamic and innovative. A couple of the staff struggled to adjust to their new positions while others were delighted. After a few months went by, even those who had difficulty adjusting thought it was a good idea and did not want to go back to the way things were. Word got out in the organization that this small unit was a very happening place to work. This encouraged dynamic staff from the organization who were looking for challenges to apply to work there. Like the flexibility-building exercise used in this organization, the beginning of your own change process will be the most difficult. It is important to stick with it for a long enough period so that change becomes second nature, and you can look forward to it. Your ability to become more flexible will depend on where you are now, to some extent. However, even if you are very inflexible, with time and effort you will learn to no longer dread the thought of change as you once did.

"Change has considerable psychological impact on the human mind. To the fearful it is threatening because it means that things may get worse. To the hopeful it is encouraging because things may get better. To the confident it is inspiring because the challenge exists to make things better."

—BUSINESSMAN KING WHITNEY, JR.

Techniques to Increase Flexibility

- **Practice making changes daily.** Take a different route to work. Take your coffee break at a different time, with a different coworker. Try something totally different for lunch. Pick things that are uncomfortable and require you to stretch, but do not cause a great deal of stress.

- **Be aware of what you tell yourself and how you feel when thinking about doing something different that makes you uncomfortable.** Challenge the things that you tell yourself. How many messages are based on evidence or reality, and how many are based on unwarranted fears? Whenever you try something new and none of the negative outcomes that you imagined occur, write it down in a book. Keep track of the number of times you do this in a week. Next week, try to increase that number.

- **Celebrate every time you try something new that is a stretch for you.** Think about how it feels to have broken through your old barriers. Share the good news, but only with those people you know will be supportive.

- **Ask for support from those you are close to who will not only be supportive but will also challenge you to reach your goals.**

- **While taking small steps to make changes on a regular basis, set goals at regular intervals.** Six-month time periods are ideal. Establish goals that are difficult for you, yet achievable. For example, let's say you are afraid of public speaking. On a daily or weekly basis, speak up in small groups more; initiate conversation with others more. All this would be leading up to you making a formal presentation to a small group.

o **Keep going. Once you have reached goals, celebrate and set higher goals.**

o **Mark into your day-timer or calendar a yearly date at which time you will review your progress.** Ask someone who is supportive, knows you well, and will give you an honest answer, if they have seen any change in you.

o **If you do not reach your goals, don't punish yourself, but do set goals you are more likely to reach.**

o **Ask others to give you examples of where they feel you could be more flexible.** What area of inflexibility do you feel is most detrimental to you? Focus on that area in your goal setting and change your plan.

Note

1. Robert Sternberg, *Successful Intelligence* (New York: Simon & Schuster), p. 153.

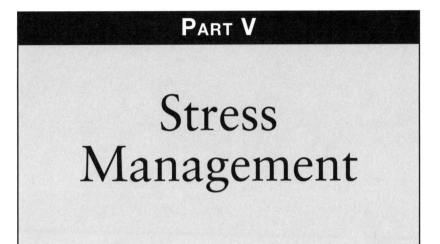

PART V

Stress
Management

CHAPTER 16

Stress Tolerance

"Reality is the leading cause of stress amongst
those in touch with it."

—COMEDIAN LILY TOMLIN

"Rule number one is, don't sweat the small stuff.
Rule number two is, it's all small stuff."

—DR. ROBERT S. ELIOT, CARDIOLOGIST

Stress results from the demands placed on us by our environment. Possible triggers of stress surround us and generally cannot be avoided. As the rate of change in our world increases constantly, there are more and more demands placed on us by our need to adapt to the world. On top of that we have to deal with ongoing pressures from our family, work, friends, and an infinite variety of other sources.

How We Experience Stress

It is sometimes easier to describe the symptoms of stress than to describe the thing itself. Some signals that we are stressed are knots in our stomach, clenched fists, and a pinched facial expression. Here is a list of the most common indicators of high stress levels:

- Forgetting things more often

- Putting off things you used to get to quickly

- Often feeling angry and agitated

- Loss of interest in friends, sex, job, and/or social activities

- Having trouble concentrating

- Restlessness; can't seem to relax; not sure what to do next

- Having a hard time falling asleep; waking in the middle of the night

- Don't feel like talking much

Stress affects all of us differently. While one person may be highly agitated sitting in busy traffic, the person in the vehicle next to him or her may be totally relaxed, sitting back and listening to some cool jazz on the radio. Why does one person get very upset in a situation that barely registers on the distress scale of another? What do the relaxed people know, do, or tell themselves that helps them to not get flustered in a tense situation? The ability to handle stress is not something we are born with, it is learned. We can all learn techniques to help us alleviate the negative effects of stress in our lives.

Positive Stress

Stress is not all bad. Psychologists tell us that some stress is a good thing and can act to motivate and cause us to take action. If we turn stress into an ally, it can help us by giving us the necessary boost of energy we need to meet and overcome challenges. Some individuals seem to thrive on stress, and seek out opportunities in their work and hobbies to push their limits. Air traffic controllers are a group that operates under stress constantly. Surgeons are another group who, under a great deal of pressure when they are working, function like professional athletes. Without any stress, our lives would be very boring. Everything we do that we feel passionate about causes us some stress. Our bodies are unable to distinguish between positive and negative stress. For example, a happy situation such as a wedding, anniversary, or major celebration causes stress for the persons directly involved. Even though this is seen as good stress, the body experiences it in the same manner as stress created by an unpleasant event. Whenever we prepare ourselves to do something that we are passionate about we feel stress. Every time I get in front of an audience to speak, even though I'm pumped and feel passionate about what I'm talking about, I feel some stress. If it ever gets to the point that I don't experience some level of anxiety while doing it, I will stop, I will know that the passion is gone and I'm only going through the motions. Stress gives us juice and the motivation to act in areas that we feel a great deal of passion about.

When Stress Becomes a Problem

The problem results when our stress levels exceed our coping and managing abilities. If stress levels become too high in our lives, the result can be burnout. We frequently hear the term *burnout* and associate it with certain helping professions such as nurses and social workers, who have to deal with people's problems every day. But it can occur in any profession and in any life situation as well.

Our physical reaction to stress is similar to that seen in the animal world. When animals sense a threat, their heart rate increases and all their senses become focused on the immediate situation. There are only two possible decisions they can make in response to the danger: fight or flight. Likewise, in humans, our initial reaction is fight or flight. Very quickly, however, our coping mechanisms come into play. It is the effectiveness of these coping mechanisms, which we can all master, that determines how effectively we deal with stress.

Stages in the Stress Cycle

There are a number of techniques that will work for reducing stress, and I will get into them at the end of this chapter. It is important, though, to realize that there are different stages in the stress cycle and the things that I will talk about will be most effective if used in the initial stage. Stages 2 and 3 will require more drastic personal changes.

Stage 1: In this stage we experience irritability, anxiousness, and anger. In this stage, we are quite aware of our emotions and can significantly decrease our levels of stress by looking after our needs. If we ignore the signals at this level, we can move to Stage 2.

Stage 2: In this stage we start to feel tired. Our attitude begins to become more negative and cynical. We start to experience periods of moodiness and depression and may have problems falling asleep. At this point, we may need to make more long-term lifestyle changes and take stress management seriously.

Stage 3: If stress is left unchecked and accumulates over a long period of time, it can lead to serious issues such as depression. At this stage, people make drastic changes in their lives such as giving up their job or their relationship(s) and changing their lives. Suicide becomes a risk. At this point, the person needs to seek professional help and get away from the situation, at least for a brief period of time.

Breaking the Stress Cycle

Like all conditions that affect us negatively, it is best to discover stress early and deal with it. When we become aware of stress early on, before it gets to the point that it immobilizes us, we have many options to help us decrease it. By learning coping techniques early on, it will keep the stress from increasing and will help us develop ways of alleviating stress in all situations that we come across. For me, the ways that reduce stress the best involve action such as doing aquasize at the local pool, or going for long walks with my dogs. This works better for me than using more sedentary techniques such as meditation. Find the system that works best for you.

If you become aware that you are more stressed than normal over a situation that is ongoing in your life, act on it immediately. Schedule a regular activity that works for you to reduce stress and start on it right away. You may find yourself continuing the activity even though you start to feel more relaxed. This is a good thing, as it will help alleviate stress buildup in the future. Prevention is the best way to deal with stress, so it is important to establish good stress-busting routines and stick to them.

> "If you are distressed by anything external, the pain is not due to the thing itself, but your estimate of it, and this you have the power to revoke any moment."
>
> —EMPEROR MARCUS AURELIUS ANTONIUS

Anita's Story

Anita thought the day would never end. She was run off of her feet, trying to cope with another of her staff members not showing up for work without giving her any notice. It didn't help that she was feeling very angry and disappointed. This seemed to further drain her energy, although anger was about the only thing that seemed to keep her going. As the owner of a small deli-style restaurant, she could only afford to pay her staff a bit above the minimum wage. This created constant problems with hiring qualified people and a high staff turnover. The types of people who were looking for this kind of work were often unmotivated and unreliable, had poor people skills, and required constant supervision. This caused Anita continuing grief and stress.

Anita was a hard worker, creative, and determined to make her business successful. She needed to make a go of the deli in order to support herself and her two children, both in their early teens and still at home with her. Daunted by the task of running the business and looking after the children on her own, she put almost all of her energy into work and home. After putting in a long day at work, she rushed home to prepare a meal for her children and look after the house. In her fear and guilt, she had given up doing the things that had helped her deal with stress in the past.

On the evening that one of her promising employees let her down by not showing up, Anita went home tired and haggard. Needing someone to talk to other than her children, she called a friend she had not seen for a long time. Her friend listened to her tales of woe and, claiming that she had nothing to do for the next couple of days, offered to help her out at the deli. Surprised at the offer, Anita was nevertheless quite proud and would have turned the generous offer down, but she was desperate and at the end of her rope.

Over the next couple of days, Anita and Ursula did a lot of talking. Ursula told her that she had already made a significant step toward dealing with her stress by reaching out for help.

The support and knowledge she gained during her conversations with Ursula were enough to give her the boost she needed to commit to a plan to deal with her stress and stave off emotional collapse. Realizing that her children needed to start helping out more around the house and with meal preparations, she sat them down and drew up a list of weekly duties for which they would be responsible. Since they were in their early teens, she was surprised that they readily accepted the challenge. Her daughter Janine told her that they were starting to worry about her, and it was a relief to her and her brother that they were able to help relieve some of the pressure. Janine even volunteered to come to the deli after school and help with some of the baking for the next day.

Anita designated an hour every evening as her time, a time when she could do her own thing and not be disturbed by the children. She would light a candle, draw herself a bubble bath, and prepare to let go of all her worldly problems. To get herself relaxed she would do some deep breathing exercises. Anita had always loved to dance and made a point of getting out every weekend with a couple of her friends.

In her deli the situation with staffing didn't get much better, but Anita tried to constantly remind herself that the people she hired would not have the same kind of commitment to the business that she did. This helped her let go of some expectations and she found herself becoming more tolerant of her staff. Before, whenever she saw one of her employees standing around, waiting at the till when there was no customer there and other work to be done, she would get quite angry. At times, she became so angry that she did not feel like talking to them. By the time she did, she would come across as irate. Often the employee would become annoyed right back, or worse, not say anything but bring it out in a passive-aggressive manner by avoiding her, or being rude and belligerent toward customers. Now, if an employee is causing Anita stress, she takes some time out to think of other things and refocus before approaching them. She finds herself less angry and the staff members have responded by being less defensive and more open to her feedback.

Although life is still a struggle and there are periods of rough water, there are now periods of peace and tranquility for Anita.

"Adopting the right attitude can convert a negative stress into a positive one."

—Dr. Hans Selye

Techniques for Reducing Stress

- **Go for walks in nature.** Focus on your surroundings and listen for the sounds of birds and other animals. Pay attention to the smells and colors.

- **Get a tape of nature sounds and listen to it regularly. Purchase a water fountain or aquarium with fish.** The sound of water is very relaxing.

- **Learn some basic meditation techniques.** Lie down or sit where you are comfortable and won't be disturbed. Take turns visualizing that your toes are getting heavy, then your ankles, feet, and legs. Work your way up to relax every portion of your body, one part at a time. Practice deep breathing, drawing in breath slowly from your abdomen.

- **Get a pet.** Dogs and cats that are affectionate and like attention are a good choice. Stroking and petting soft, furry animals is very relaxing.

- **Spend time with hobbies and activities in which you can totally engross yourself.** If you love music, take time to lose yourself in your pieces. If you love working with your hands, take on a project that requires your entire attention.

- **Go to one funny movie or play.** Share some laughs with friends. Think of humorous situations and stories you can share with them. See who can come up with the funniest story of the evening.

CHAPTER 17

Impulse Control

"A true history of human events would show that
a far larger proportion of our acts are the result of
sudden impulses and accident than of reason
of which we so often boast."

—ALBERT COOPER, BRITISH PARLIAMENTARIAN

The importance of impulse control in our lives can be demonstrated by an experiment that was conducted on a group of four-year-olds at Stanford University in the early 1960s. Placed in a room, the four-year-olds had a marshmallow placed in front of each one of them. The adults then told the children that they were going to leave the room for ten minutes. The children were also told that when the adults came back, the children who still had their marshmallow would get another one. Ten minutes is a long time for four-year-olds to sit and stare at a marshmallow and not eat it. About one-third of the children gobbled up the marshmallow right away. Some waited a little longer. Some licked the marshmallow; some took little nibbles but resisted the temptation. About one-third of the kids were able to hold out and were rewarded with an extra marshmallow. Since the parents of the children were all university professors, who tended not to move very often, it was relatively easy to do follow-up research on them.

The children were divided into two groups and compared on a number of different levels when they reached high school. Very real differences were found between how well the two groups were functioning. The ones who had eaten their marshmallow first were having markedly more problems at school and home compared with the group that resisted giving in to their impulse. The marshmallow resisters had the habits of successful people. On a personal level they were more positive, persistent in the face of difficulty, self-motivating, and continued to demonstrate an ability to delay gratification. Their incomes were higher, their marriages more successful, and they had better health, greater career satisfaction, and more fulfilling lives than most people. The ones who immediately ate their marshmallow, on the other hand, were having a great deal of difficulty in many areas of their lives. They tended to be more indecisive, stubborn, and mistrustful, less self-confident, and continued to have problems delaying gratification. This resulted in low job satisfaction, troubled marriages, low incomes, bad health, and frustrating lives.

An Unchecked Mouth

There have likely been more careers stalled and opportunities lost on the job due to people saying the wrong thing at the wrong time than for any other reason. One outburst of unchecked anger has often come back to haunt the person who exploded. Likewise, saying hurtful things in a fit of rage and anger can permanently damage relationships with those close to us. We have all said and done things when angry that we wish we could take back. Often it is too late because the damage has been done.

This is not a problem that affects only us ordinary folks. Think of all of the celebrities and politicians whose careers and reputations have been permanently damaged, or totally ruined, by shooting off at the mouth before their brain was actively engaged.

Unchecked Spending

Impulse buying creates financial hardship and ruin for thousands of North Americans. Instead of saving money for a larger home or a nicer car many opt for the instant gratification fix and overextend themselves on their mortgages and car loans. Although corporate greed and the banks are often blamed for this practice, it would not have been possible without large numbers of people who were unwilling to delay gratification. While the lending institutions invariably take advantage of people's gullibility, the unmanageable debt wouldn't happen if consumers had the ability to wait until they could afford their homes or cars, or make due with homes they could afford.

Impulse Control and Spontaneity

Sometimes low impulse control can be confused with spontaneity and flexibility, which are good attributes to have. Let me give you an example, which I hope will demonstrate the difference. One evening you and a friend are taking your car out to get it washed. On the way back, you suddenly decide that you have a craving for a double fudge sundae and, unannounced, pull into a Dairy Queen. Your friend thinks it's a good idea and decides that he would like one as well. That is spontaneity. It is fun and there are no potential serious negative consequences. People who are spontaneous and flexible are normally fun to be with, as they are open to trying new things, changing plans, and doing things on the spur of the moment. This breaks up routine and adds spice to life.

Take the same situation with another ending. You and your friend are returning home after washing your car and on the way pass a car dealership. In the driveway, you spot a red sports car that grabs your attention. You turn into the lot, and after getting behind the steering wheel, you decide you must have it. Your friend, who is rather immature and not looking out for your best interests, dares you to buy it. Buying it will put you into serious financial hardship. You are married with two small children and are barely able to make the mortgage payments on the house that you bought six months ago. However, the thought of how cool you will look in your new toy overwhelms you, and the salesman soon has your signature on the sales contract. You now have to go home and explain this to your spouse, who is already stressed out over the family finances. This is a lack of impulse control. Had you thought through all the consequences of making the decision, you likely would not have bought the car.

The Ten-Second Method

Simply counting to ten before speaking or acting is likely the easiest and best advice to give someone who suffers from impulse control problems, as it allows time for our thinking process to start. The counting to ten practice has proven effective in anger management programs and will work for impulse control just as well. Once we start to think, our reactions will be muted or changed so that the chances of saying or doing something we will later regret significantly decrease.

I use the counting to ten practice myself whenever I get into situations where I find myself being hijacked by my emotions. Several months ago, I was driving along in the right lane of a three-lane street in the city. It was early in the afternoon and the traffic was fairly light. Suddenly a car cut directly in front of me, causing me to slow down suddenly. Angry, my first impulse was to blow my horn to show him that I was unhappy with his behavior. My first thoughts were that the driver was a selfish person, who, realizing he had to turn right at the last minute was prepared to slow down all the traffic in my lane, and risk an accident just so he would not have to go a few extra blocks to get to where he was going. Instead of giving in to my impulse to let him know how much I disapproved of his behavior, I started counting to ten. As I started to count, I noticed that he had not signaled a right turn. Still thinking that he intended to turn right I considered that his not signaling was just another indication of his inconsideration for others. By the time I counted to ten, however, my anger had gone down and I no longer had the urge to blow the horn. I was by now more curious than anything, wondering what he was going to do next. Then I heard the siren. An ambulance was coming down the center lane. Instead of being the selfish jerk that I originally thought he was, the driver, having seen the ambulance before I did, was getting out of the way. Imagine how I would have felt had I given in to my first impulse? It could have been worse. In a moment of anger I could have swerved into the left lane, right into the path of the upcoming ambulance.

Road rage incidents are becoming a serious issue on U.S. highways and are taking their toll on our health, finances, and emotional well-being. It seems that people feel invincible surrounded by their automobiles and it becomes safe to let out their frustrations. This frequently results in tragic consequences with situations erupting into violence, resulting in people being seriously injured, even killed. Fortunately, armed with a few simple techniques, most people can overcome the first destructive temptations that cause escalations in road rage incidents that lead to a destructive ending.

Dealing with Emotions on the Spot

Unless we are able to find ways of effectively dealing with everyday frustrations effectively on the spot, the effects will carry over into other areas of our lives. Still feeling frustrated and angry over an incident on the way to work, we might take our frustrations out at our boss, coworkers, employees, or customers. Becoming angry over an incident before we leave work can result in us snapping at our wives, husbands, partners, children, and pets. When I'm aware that I'm still carrying strong emotions from work to home, I sit in my car for a few minutes, close my eyes, get centered, and breathe from my abdomen. I concentrate on releasing the anger from my body. When I feel calm, collected, and centered I head toward the house. If time doesn't allow for this, as when I have a meeting or appointment that I will be late for, I breathe deeply, releasing negative energy as I am walking from the parking lot to my work site.

> "For in truth we who are creatures of impulse are creatures of despair."
>
> —AUTHOR JOSEPH CONRAD

Shaun's Story

When it came to obtaining a job and advancing in it, Shaun was his own worst enemy. It wasn't a lack of ability, talent, or opportunity that held him back. He had a university degree and was considered to be a bright guy by those who knew him. But impulsive outbursts at inappropriate times had cost him opportunities for job promotions and even came out at times during interviews.

After years of underemployment, Shaun had an opportunity to get a position in the human resources field in which he had been trained. Since he was basically qualified, he got an interview. The job was in a small town—a two-hour drive from the city in which he lived. He knew his chances of getting a job in a small office were better because they had problems recruiting and keeping qualified people.

Shaun got the job. This was the break that he so badly needed and had wished for. Now the challenge was to stay positive and avoid the impulsive anger episodes that had cost him so dearly in the past.

It wasn't long before Shaun was put to the test. The company was part of a large conglomerate that had branches in all major cities, including his own. Shaun was hoping to transfer back to his home-town, and the sooner the better. He had kept his home in the city and rented a place in the small town, where he stayed in during the week. On weekends, which he lived for, he came back to the city.

Within a month of starting his new job, Shaun saw a job posting on his e-mail at work for a position with his company back in his hometown. Seeing an opportunity to get back there he applied immediately. The next day his manager, Steven, called him into his office. "So I hear you're applying for a job back in Tucson," he said. "We've got you for a year. I understand you wanting to transfer back home, but we have to train you and everything." Shaun had not been told anything about the one-year rule, and it had not been in the contract he had signed when he started to work. The first thought that came to mind was that this was a bunch of BS, and how could they get away with this?

In the past, he would have gotten angry and confronted his boss about the company having a hidden agenda. Not this time, however. Shaun waited until his anger began to fade, and then forced his thoughts back to what his purpose was for being there and what he needed to come away with in this situation. He concentrated on the fact that he would need Steven's support and reference to have a chance of getting a transfer back to Tucson. Hiding his anger and disappointment, he told Steven that he hadn't realized he was expected to be there a year but he understood the reasons for it. Steven was relieved that Shaun was taking it better than expected and joked, "It was worth a try."

Shaun had taken a very significant step in his self-improvement program. Resigned to putting in at least one year, he was now determined to make the most of the situation. Although his coworkers were friendly and supportive, they were small-town people with whom he had very little in common.

After about six months on the job, Shaun's new impulse control skills were about to be put to the test again. He had been hired to carry out primarily human resources consulting work. The job had been advertised as such and his job description stated it, although part of his duties was helping with administrative tasks whenever the need arose. This need, he had been led to believe, was to cover for holidays and helping out during brief, busy periods. This he had been prepared for and accepted as part of working in a small office. Up to this point, his work had been going well. Janet, his direct supervisor, was seldom around and left him alone to do his job. He appreciated the independence of not having anyone constantly watching over his shoulder.

Then one day Janet dropped a bombshell on him. Shaun was to start doing administrative duties half-time. The administrative employee had developed a health issue that required her to work only part-time. This added insult to injury. First Shaun had been unjustly forced to stay in his job and denied the right to relocate. Now they were going to make him do something that clearly was outside of his job description. Although he was unable to put on fake enthusiasm, at least Shaun did not show his anger directly to his supervisor. Again, he forced himself to take time out before speaking. He thought of his goals, which were to get out of there as soon as possible. To do this, he realized, he needed his supervisor even more than the manager, since the supervisor would surely be asked for a reference on him prior to his obtaining a transfer.

When he thought about it, Shaun realized he had two choices. First, he could carry out his new administrative duties grudgingly, complaining the whole time. This would likely upset his supervisor, who would end up giving him a bad reference and ensure that he would not be getting a transfer any time soon. On the other hand, if he carried out his new duties at least without complaining, he might warrant a favorable reference. Since he would have to do the work in either scenario, thought Shaun, he might as well use it to his advantage. Shaun found that when he was able to give up resentment and anger over his situation, the time he spent at work became more pleasant.

Once Shaun's year was drawing to a close, he started to look at opportunities back in Tucson. He had a couple of interviews but was unsuccessful. Then a position came up that he not only had a strong interest in but it offered a promotion as well. The interview seemed to go well. Shaun had done his homework and was prepared. A few days later, he had a question for his supervisor. The door to Janet's office was open as he approached. She was talking to someone on the phone. He heard her say, "He's really a good team player." At this point she saw him, said something to the person she was talking to, and got up to close the door, sheepishly apologizing to Shaun, telling him she was having a private conversation.

It took him a few minutes to realize that she was in the process of giving him a reference. Embarrassed, his supervisor later confirmed to him that this was what he had interrupted. Shaun started to get his hopes up, knowing that all the signs were there telling him that he had a good chance of not only getting back home but into a more rewarding job. The next day his phone rang. On the display screen he could see that the call was coming from his company's personnel office in Tucson. His heart began to race. Taking a deep breath he picked up the phone, trying not to sound too excited or eager. The voice on the other end offered him the job.

It was all he could do not to scream at the top of his lungs that yes, of course he would take it. When he hung up the phone his first impulse was to go running down the aisles, pumping his fist in the air and shouting, "YES! YES! YES!" He resisted the impulse to do it, since taking the mandatory time out to think about it made him realize that some of his coworkers might not share his joy. They had treated him well and it occurred to him that some might take this eagerness to leave their work site as a personal repudiation of them. Instead he sat there for a long time . . . just savoring the moment. God, but it felt great! The monster within that had caused him to miss so many opportunities in the past was finally safely behind bars . . . and he held the key!

"If I ever marry it will be on a sudden impulse—as a man shoots himself."

—H. L. MENCKEN, AMERICAN JOURNALIST, ESSAYIST, MAGAZINE EDITOR, SATIRIST, AND ACERBIC CRITIC OF AMERICAN LIFE AND CULTURE

Techniques to Reduce Destructive Impulses

- Practice counting to ten before reacting to any strong feelings with potential negative consequences.

- Wait until you feel you are in control of your words before speaking.

- If you have to, physically leave the situation.

- Think of situations when you got angry and the situation was not what you thought it was. For example, the other day while I was in a public restroom, someone kept trying the door, even though it was obviously locked. I found myself starting to get angry. My first reaction would have been to shout out, "What is your problem? Can't you tell that someone's in here!" When I thought about it, however, I came to the conclusion that a normal person would not act in that manner. Upon exiting, I saw that the person on the other side had a mental disability, and I was grateful for not having given in to my first impulse.

o **Find someone or a group where it is safe to release anger and other strong feelings.** There are a couple of organizations listed at the end of this book for both men and women that welcome and work with emotions.

o **Whenever you feel your emotions slipping away, think of a goal, something positive you want to leave the situation with.**

o **Use poor impulsive decisions you've made to your advantage.** You can do this by remembering them whenever you find yourself tempted to be destructively impulsive.

o **Post a sticky note for yourself somewhere that you see daily (on your mirror in the bathroom or the dash of your car).** The note should say something along the lines of "Whenever I find myself tempted I will remember the time I _____."

o **Reward yourself for not giving in to a strong negative emotion by doing something for yourself you would not normally do.**

o **Ask trusted family members or friends to confront you if they see that you are about to act impulsively.**

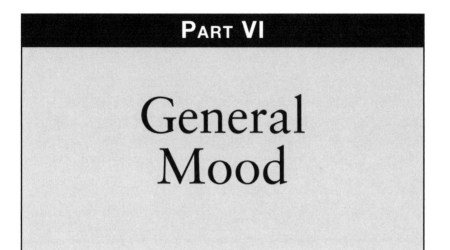

PART VI

General Mood

CHAPTER 18

Happiness

"The secret of happiness is this: Let your interests be
as wide as possible, and let your reactions to the things
and persons that interest you be as far as possible
friendly rather than hostile."

—BERTRAND RUSSELL, BRITISH PHILOSOPHER,
MATHEMATICIAN, AND NOBEL LAUREATE

Are you happy? This has got to be one of the most basic questions of life, one we have asked and been asked many times. We all think we understand happiness, but do we really? Do we know when we are feeling joy? Are we able to truly tell if those we are close to are happy?

At the end of the day, when all is said and done, happiness seems to be the most important thing. After all, if in the end we don't have it, what does the rest matter? Americans are so enthralled with the idea of happiness that they enshrined the right to pursue it in the U.S. Constitution. Why is it that even though we have material wealth, which is the envy of millions who are less fortunate, many of us are discontent? In North America, despite the fact that people's income has substantially increased over the last forty years, there is no corresponding increase in happiness. Up to 25 percent of Americans at any given time claim that they are depressed. Less than 30 percent of Americans claim that they are very happy.

The Secret? There Is No Secret

There is no real secret to finding happiness. It isn't found in some magic formula that some people seem to have discovered and others have not. All of the studies that have been done on joyful people have come up with the same basic answers. A part of our happiness is determined by our genes. We are brought up with an inherent level of happiness that we inherit when we are born. Estimates are that that makes up about 50 percent of our happiness level. Our happiness is preset at a certain level and even though events in our lives can change that level, within a couple of years we seem to return to that level. There seems to be no difference as to whether that event boosts our happiness or diminishes it. Lottery winners who won large sums of money became happier over a short period of time after winning, but within a couple of years were back to the level they were at before. The same held true for people who had the misfortune of becoming confined to wheelchairs. It was also found that within a couple of years they had returned to their previous happiness level.

Qualities of Happiness

Dan Baker, the director of the Life Enhancement Program at Canyon Ranch, has experienced what makes people happy firsthand. In his book, *What Happy People Know*, he has this to say:

> You can't just decide to be happy any more than you can decide to be taller. That's because happiness is not a finite entity unto itself, but is the sum of the twelve most important qualities of happiness: love, optimism, courage, a sense of freedom, proactivity, security, health, spirituality, altruism, perspective, humor, and purpose. These are the things you should make up your mind to achieve.
>
> One of the ways that we can develop these qualities is to do things that make us feel good. Whenever we do something that makes us feel good, we are more receptive to all of the qualities that lead to happiness. Often the thing that makes me feel

good is giving attention to my two apricot poodles, Buddy and Korky. I can spend hours sitting on the sofa, one of the poodles curled up on each side of me enjoying being scratched or getting massaged. The other thing that makes me happy is my writing. When I get excited about explaining something that I feel is important, I find myself becoming totally engrossed in it.

Find things that engross you, that take all of your focus and attention. Look for opportunities to do more of the things that totally engross you and always be on the lookout for new things to try that you think you may enjoy. Think of a song that makes you feel good, better yet sing an upbeat happy song or tune. Always be open to new experiences as we are not always a good judge of whether we will enjoy something until we try it. Keep an open mind to all new experiences. See exploring sources of happiness as an adventure."[1]

Mental Habits of the Happy

Marci Shimoff found one hundred of the happiest people and studied them to determine what they had in common. She discovered that: "Instead of being overrun with negative thoughts or constantly going into fight-or-flight mode, happy people have habits that allow them to respond more easily from their higher brain center, the neo-cortex. From my interviews with the Happy 100, I've found that they don't believe everything they think."[2] According to her research, happy people also tend not to take their negative thoughts verbatim but question their validity while making an effort to rise above them. They don't spend a lot of time and energy wrestling with their negative thoughts, as they are confident that they will be able to rise above them and those thoughts will pass. Happy people tend to get into their positive thoughts and squeeze out every ounce of joy.

Every time we catch ourselves having a negative thought, we should get into the habit of trying to find something positive in the situation to focus on. At first this may seem like a lot of work, but after a while it will become automatic. It will limit the amount of time and energy that we spend time on the negative. If you are unable to do this at times, simply try to let the thought go. Try to focus on something else, such as:

- A favorite piece of music.

- A good time that you had with family or friends.

- Noticing something in your environment and ask yourself questions about it. For example, if you find yourself angry about something when driving, notice the cars around you. Which one stands out for you? What makes it stand out? Imagine yourself driving one.

Don't struggle to find a positive thought if one doesn't come immediately, just focus on something that is neutral. Some people have an elastic band on their wrists and snap it whenever they find themselves having negative thoughts. This helps to break the thought for the moment and makes it easier to move on to a thought that is positive.

On the other hand, draw out positive thoughts as much as you can. Focus on them and build on them by thinking of other positive experiences when these begin to wane. Although it is difficult to constantly monitor what we think about, our feelings are a good indicator of the kinds of thoughts we are having. If we are feeling good, the thoughts will be positive ones.

The Magic of Focus

In his book *Flow*, Mihaly Csikszentmihalyi writes that there is a close connection between happiness and concentration. He set up a research study that grew to encompass more than ten thousand people over a twenty-five year period. Subjects in the research study were paged at random and asked to rate their level of happiness whenever the pagers were activated. It was found that the more immersed the subjects were in whatever task they were doing, the higher was their level of happiness. Curiously, the subjects were not always able to predict which activity would make them happy. However, it was found that whenever they were totally involved in something and the pager brought them out of their concentration, they realized that they had been very happy doing the activity. From his lengthy research, Csikszentmihalyi concluded that happiness was strongly linked to focus and rarely could we be happy unless we were also focused. Another interesting conclusion that he came to was that we only experience happiness after the event is completed. While we are deeply immersed in whatever the event is that is bringing us happiness, we are too focused to be aware that we are happy. We can only enjoy the happiness from the experience after it has occurred.

Happiness Comes from Within

Many people feel that they will be happy when they buy that new house, find that great partner, get that new car, or get that job promotion. Once these things come about, they feel that they will be truly happy. Others think that they will find happiness in addictive behaviors such as alcohol and gambling. What that does is temporarily numb the pain of unhappiness. When the addiction wears off they find themselves no happier than before. It has been discovered by researchers that about 50 percent of our happiness is genetic. Apparently we are born with a certain predisposition to happiness. Research has shown us, however, that things outside of ourselves, such as material possessions and relationships with others make up only a small percentage of our overall happiness, less than 10 percent. That leaves up to 40 percent of happiness that we create from within. And we can create it if we keep the following things in mind.

- **We choose how we react to all situations.** As Victor Frankl, a concentration camp survivor, demonstrated, we have ultimate control over how we choose to react in all situations. Even in the midst of the horror of a concentration camp, he was able to find examples of human kindness and decency. He was able to find enough positives to allow him to struggle on every day and survive. One of the ways we can cultivate looking for the positive is to keep a gratitude book. At the end of every day, write down all the things you have to be grateful for that day. The more we think of the things we are grateful for, the easier it will be to react positively in all situations.

○ **Anyone can be happy when things are going right; it takes a great deal of emotional intelligence to laugh when things are not going well.** In good times, even a pessimist can find something to be thankful for. However, during difficult times it is easy for those whose predominant thoughts are negative to fall back into negative thinking patterns. This is where daily habits of gratitude will make all the difference. During difficult times, those who are used to being positive and experiencing good feelings will have a large pool to draw from. It is in difficult times where we will see the real benefits of consistently building up our positive thoughts and gratitude. Those practices will sustain us over difficult periods. Optimists as well will be able to say "This too shall pass" as their belief is that the universe is basically good and difficult times are only temporary.

○ **Don't underestimate the power that one person has to change the mood of others around them.** Have you ever watched a powerful speaker control a crowd, bringing forth powerful emotions such as joy, fear, and anger? Many powerful orators have been able to whip huge crowds of people into a frenzy. Yet, we all have tremendous capability for influencing the mood of others around us. Have you ever experienced one negative person dragging down the mood of a group of people in a room? On the other hand, have you seen a room get brighter and livelier when an upbeat positive person speaks? Become a person who brightens up a room when you enter. If you have ever experienced this, you will know what a wonderful and powerful feeling this is.

"What a wonderful life I've had! I only wish I'd realized it sooner."

—French Novelist Colette

Yip's Story

One of the bad habits that I have been working at breaking is my tendency to exceed the speed limit when driving within city limits. Because of this behavior, I've taken many trips to the local courthouse. Despite my best efforts at explaining to the judge the unique circumstances of my situation, guilty is the usual verdict. After the courtroom experience, there is the matter of standing in the fine payment lineup waiting for the next available cashier. There is a ritual that goes along with this. Often people in these lines like to share their frustrations with the other unfortunate souls in the same situation. Nobody is ever happy to be there. The atmosphere of the place is somber; rarely is anyone smiling or laughing.

The cashier at the fine-paying desk is the first person they see after their hearing, and she is taking their hard-earned money. Naturally, there will be a lot of misdirected anger and frustration directed toward these people. There had apparently been enough problems that a couple of signs had been erected. They stated: "ZERO TOLERANCE: Swearing, cursing, or raising your voice will not be tolerated at this work site. If you engage in these behaviors, staff will refuse to serve you."

Recently, I was standing in line at the local courthouse waiting to pay a speeding ticket. Ahead of me in front of the cashier's wicket was a small Asian man. He was laughing, and continued to laugh, as he rolled off the bills to pay his fine. Everyone stopped what they were doing and stared. Likely some thought he must be drunk, high on something, or "not all there." Before leaving he said, "Now I'm free." Being the next person in line, I went to take his spot. The cashier was one who had served me before. If her expression could be translated into words, it would say, "Don't give me any crap, don't tell me any stories, do your business as quickly as possible, and get the hell out of my face!"

Today, however, there was a strange expression on her face. It almost looked as if there was a smile developing on her face, a little forced maybe, but a smile all the same. Noticing the change, I worked up my courage and approached her in a different manner. I remarked to the cashier that I had never seen anyone so happy about paying a fine. We both got a chuckle out of this, and I joked that there was no place to include a tip on the charge card slip that I had to sign. By this time she was in good humor, her smile broad, open, and relaxed. A complete stranger had infected us both, making our business both fun and pleasant, and brightening our day. Walking away I had the feeling that this was a very special moment, the type that rarely occurs in our lives. When it does, it happens for a purpose.

I had no way of knowing fate had decided that I would meet the stranger in a line that turned around the mood of at least two people that fateful day.

It is quite common for me to work after hours in my office. Often the janitors come around and clean around me as I'm working away. I noticed that they were almost all foreigners, probably recent immigrants who likely would have trouble finding other types of employment. When I tried to strike up basic conversations with them, they responded in very broken English. One day I noticed a slight, short, Asian gentleman, whom I had not seen before. "I've seen him somewhere before," I thought. Suddenly, it occurred to me that he was the man in line at the courthouse. Fascinated by this turn of events, I tried to make small talk with him. Whatever it was that made this man tick, I vowed to find out.

Over a period of time we began chatting on a regular basis. Knowing that he would be coming in, I'd put on a pot of coffee and ask him to take a break and join me. Slowly he overcame his shyness and reservations and began to share tidbits of his past with me.

Eventually, after months had passed, I felt comfortable enough around Yip to tell him that I had been in line on the day he paid his fine and witnessed his interaction with the cashier. To explain, he talked about what it had been like at home. Yip had come from Vietnam, one of the boat people who risked their lives in open seas, crowded into the rusty hulks of anything that floated, for a chance at freedom and a new life. In southern Vietnam he had been a schoolteacher. After the Communists took over, he was forced to teach a lot of things he did not believe in. Yip had been imprisoned for continuing to teach his students subjects that were forbidden under the Communists. When you were charged with something, you were on the authorities' blacklist forever. Records were kept on you and you were watched. Coworkers spied on you and reported any suspicious activities. Even though you did your time, and paid for whatever it was that you were accused of, you were never really free from it. In his new country it was different. When you paid your fine, you were really free.

People who are positive and happy are naturally attracted to others who are positive. You know the old saying, "Misery loves company." Do you want to attract miserable people into your life? It's easy to do—all you have to do is be miserable. On the other hand, happy people do their best to avoid miserable people. Run, don't walk, away from negative people. They will drain your energy. There is something positive in all situations that you encounter, although it may not always be clear or evident at the moment.

Unlike Yip, I could not see the positive in paying a traffic fine. His gift was in demonstrating that there is an upside to every situation if you look hard enough. Make it a habit to always look for the positive, even in situations where it is far from obvious. Challenge yourself to find something good in unpleasant situations. When you do find it, focus on it. It has been proven that we are only able to hold on to one thought at a time. Choose to think positive.

Techniques for Increasing Your Happiness

- **Keep a gratitude book.** At the end of the day, before going to bed, write down ten things that happened today that you are grateful for.

- **Volunteer to help someone less fortunate than yourself.**

- Call someone you care about and haven't seen for a while just to see how they are doing.

- Look for opportunities to compliment others on their appearance, a job well done, or a selfless act.

- Carry out random acts of kindness.

Notes

1. Dan Baker, Ph.D., *What Happy People Know, How the New Science of Happiness Can Change Your Life for the Better* (New York: St. Martin's Griffin, 2003), p. 77.
2. Marci Shimoff, *Happy for No Reason: 7 Steps to Being Happy from the Inside Out* (New York: Free Press, 2008), p. 90.

CHAPTER 19

Optimism

"Hope is definitely not the same thing as optimism. It is not the conviction that something will turn out well, but the certainty that something makes sense, regardless of how it turns out."

—VACLAV HAVEL, FORMER PRESIDENT OF THE CZECH REPUBLIC

Optimism is the ability to see hope and stay positive in all situations and times, regardless of how bleak the present may be. When things are going well, it is quite easy to be upbeat and in good spirits. Success, however, demands that we be able to see hope and possibilities even after major setbacks. One of the common denominators of all successful people is their ability to bounce back after failures. You have likely heard stories of well-known successful people and their struggle to overcome adversity. Every motivational speaker has stories about these people.

"That which does not kill us makes us stronger."

—FRIEDRICH NIETZSCHE, NINETEENTH-CENTURY GERMAN PHILOSOPHER

Failure is an essential step on the road to success. I read an article on young self-made millionaires, all under forty, who had created successful business ventures. It was found that, on the average, they had failed in about seventeen or eighteen enterprises before finding the one that made them so successful. This sounds a lot like my former dating practices. Obviously, the self-made millionaires had to have a great deal of optimism.

It is infinitely easier to be optimistic when things are going well. But what about being able to maintain a sense of optimism despite going through the worst of tragedies? Robin Sharma tells us that if we avoid pain we may be avoiding the potential for personal growth that often comes with difficulties in life. It is during these trying times that we often find we find lessons that help us stretch ourselves to another level.[1] Our most difficult struggles force us to push back our comfort zones and find resources and strengths that we never knew were there. Many great books and much wonderful music have been written when the authors and composers have been going through very difficult times in their lives. Although we may not be able to see it at the time, there is an inner gift that we are meant to discover when we are struggling. I found that gift when I was unemployed a number of years ago. Frustrated and feeling very vulnerable I put all of my energy into writing, something I had always felt a desire to do but had not seriously pursued. Up to that point, I had not found anything that I felt strongly enough about that I felt it needed to be said. My struggles with unemployment provided me with the impetus that I needed to seriously get going with my writing and it changed my entire life. I managed to complete the book and find a publisher. This brought me a tremendous amount of satisfaction and for the first time I began to see my true potential. A painful experience forced me to discover and develop my courage, perseverance, imagination, and initiative.

How Optimism Works

A great deal of research has been done on optimism. Although most of us would not be surprised to discover that optimistic people tend to be more successful, we might not realize that they also tend to live longer and have healthier lives.

In his book *Learned Optimism*, Martin Seligman presents a great deal of research on the differences between optimists and pessimists. What makes some people keep going after repeated setbacks, while others give up after the first sign of difficulty? It is quite natural for people to get down emotionally when they have major setbacks. Optimists, however, do not stay down. They quickly look at the situation and consider ways they can change the outcome next time.

What We Say to Ourselves

According to Seligman, how people explain events and situations to themselves determines whether or not they are optimistic. People who look on the bright side of things see setbacks as temporary instead of permanent. While they don't shirk their responsibility for things not working out, they tend to look at the broader picture and see a multitude of reasons why things went the way they did. To them, a bad situation or mistake does not mean that they are a defective, worthless person who will never get anywhere in life. If they do see that it was a shortcoming of theirs that led to the negative event or situation, they look for ways they can change their behaviors or actions in the future.

Flexibility

Being flexible is a very important part of being an optimist. The more adaptable and comfortable with change we are, the more control we feel we have over our environment. The flexible person knows that there are many ways to see a situation and solve a problem. Knowing this helps the optimist look at the future in a positive way. Flexibility allows them to have more control over their environment and shape the future in a way that serves them in the best possible manner. Inflexible people see few options and tend to see themselves as victims of circumstance and their environment. While viewing negative events and situations as temporary, optimists see their ability to learn, change, grow, and adapt as permanent and part of who they are.

Keeping It Real

Being optimistic also means having a solid grounding in reality. Trying something that has little chance of success and carries a great likelihood of negative consequences is not being optimistic; it is foolhardy. An example is someone who does no retirement planning because he believes that he is going to win the lottery. This would be very foolish, not only because the chances of winning the lottery are minuscule but also because the belief would prevent the person from taking concrete actions necessary to ensure a successful retirement.

Basking in Successes

Pessimists, on the other hand, see positive events as being a matter of luck or the result of outside influences over which they have no control. Seldom do they see the value of their own contributions. Although an optimist does not take more than her share of the responsibility for a failure, she will take her credit when things go well. This does not mean that optimists are braggarts or know-it-alls, going around telling everyone what to do and how to live their lives. They are simply people who have enough self-regard to give themselves a pat on the back when they have accomplished something worthwhile. Their self-confidence can to others sometimes appear as cockiness. How can we tell if a person is really high in self-regard or simply a blowhard trying to make himself or herself look good to others? Truly self-confident people do not have the need to put down others. They are not threatened by the achievements of others and will support them in their quest to reach their goals.

Looking for Goodness

Bestselling author Bob Nelson, in *1001 Ways to Take Initiative at Work*, has this to say about the value of optimism in the workplace. "Don't automatically assume anything negative about anybody. Instead, look for the good in everyone you meet and in everything you do. You'll be amazed at how much better your coworkers will feel about themselves when you are there to lift their spirits."[2]

There are times when it is difficult, even for the most optimistic, to see the positive in a situation. In that case, the optimists will put their energy and efforts into moving on. They will take their lumps and go on to fight another day. Optimists are the ultimate survivors.

Optimism and Success

For Robin Sharma, optimism is a crucial and essential part for all of us to be able to reach our potential. He sees the importance of optimism as often being undervalued, but argues that if we can become more optimistic it will go a long way towards overcoming our obstacles and becoming the best we can be.[3]

Goal setting is by its nature an exercise in optimism. If we did not believe that we could achieve our goals, there would be no point in setting them in the first place. Those who achieve a great deal are by nature more optimistic than those who set their goals low. High achievers set their goals high in accordance with their level of optimism. The ideals that we strive for can only be reached through setting our sights on a goal, reaching that goal, and then setting the marker higher. Just like the high jumper in gymnastics, we set our level higher every time that we reach our goals. Only through continuously testing ourselves and believing in our ability are we able to fully discover and reach the highest level that we are capable of.

> "Few things in the world are more powerful than a positive push. A smile. A word of optimism and hope. A 'you can do it' when things are tough."
>
> —AMERICAN ENTREPRENEUR RICHARD M. DeVos

Jim's Story

Jim is definitely a survivor. His story is much more than just one of survival, however; it is about coming back from adversity to renewal, faith, and hope. Jim's father was an alcoholic. From an early age he remembered being afraid of his father, especially when he was drunk and angry. Although his father was never physically abusive to Jim or any of his five brothers and sisters, the memories of fear still remain with him fifty years later. Because of the large number of children in the family, his parents had difficulty coping. It was decided that Jim, at the age of five, would go to live with his grandparents. He was torn away from his siblings and parents and remembers the feelings of loneliness and isolation. Having been the one chosen to leave the home, he felt rejected and defective. Although his grandparents treated him well, Jim missed his family and felt that he was being punished for something, even though he was never sure for what.

If there was an upside to Jim's living with his grandparents, it was that he learned to be independent. They also gave him responsibilities and a great deal more leeway in carrying out his duties than was allowed his siblings living at home. His grandparents maintained his family's tradition of attending church regularly. The thing that Jim remembers most about his grandfather was that he always looked at the bright side of life. Whenever Jim had a problem or was complaining about something, his grandfather always sat with him and talked to him as an adult. He explained that things would always get better if we believed that they would. Here was a man who had gone through some very difficult times in his life—war and economic depression—and still remained happy, cheerful, and believed that good times lay ahead. It was in church that Jim was able to find friends, a purpose, and solace from his everyday life. In his late teens, he met a girl at a camp sponsored by his church; by the time he was twenty, they were married.

Following the tradition of his working-class family, Jim went on to learn a trade and became an electrician. Although he was good at the work, he found that he had a longing to work for himself, to be independent. Within three years of becoming a full-fledged tradesman, Jim and a partner started their own small company. Because both were hardworking, ambitious, and got along well, their company flourished, providing them with an income that was double what they had previously earned while working for someone else.

By now Jim and his wife, Lynn, had three young children. Jim's company, while providing a good income for his family, was taking up an increasing amount of his time. There were always pressures and responsibilities. As well, Jim was beginning to drink more heavily. He had always enjoyed a drink, and as a teenager had a reputation among his friends for being able to handle his alcohol. While they were still dating early on, Lynn had expressed many times that she was worried about the amount he drank. He paid little attention, thinking that was what all boys his age did. Besides that, he really enjoyed drinking. The problems in his family worsened as Jim's drinking increased.

To cope, Jim spent more time at work, avoiding his family. His wife, whom he later realized he had never really been close to, distanced herself from him and put all of her focus on their children. He later came to the realization that he had suffered as much from loneliness in the relationship with Lynn as he had when he was growing up with his grandparents. What finally brought Jim to the recognition that he was an alcoholic who needed help was seeing that his children were afraid of him, just as he had been of his father. The awareness that he had become just like his father came as a major shock. It was one of those defining moments in life when the realization hits that we have to take drastic action to change direction, because we don't like what awaits us at the end of the road.

Jim joined Alcoholics Anonymous and dealt with his drinking in the same determined manner that he took on projects for his company. He thought that all of the responsibility for his marriage not working out was due to his drinking, and as soon as he stopped things would automatically get better. His faith remained a constant, always there for him when he needed it. It was, in fact, one of the few constants there was in his life.

Business kept expanding, and Jim and his partner had six full-time employees working for them. Before the age of forty, Jim was a millionaire, a self-made man. He was remaining sober, and had hopes that he could still save his crumbling marriage and develop a close relationship with his children.

One day during this period, Jim got a call from his accountant.

A check made out to a supplier had bounced, causing the accountant to investigate. Jim's partner of fourteen years had embezzled all of the money out of their joint operating account. When Jim called him at home, he discovered that the phone had been disconnected. If there was a time that Jim desperately wanted to drink, this was it. He didn't, however. Whenever he found that he was feeling sorry for himself, he thought of his grandfather who had faced situations that he imagined as much worse than he was facing and remained positive.

Without any money to pay the bills, the company was soon forced into receivership and Jim declared bankruptcy. He remembers how badly he wanted to go back to drinking during those times. He felt betrayed, angry, and yes, at times, even stupid and gullible. What made it somewhat easier for Jim to accept was that there were a lot of people who had been taken in and swindled by his partner. These people, he told himself, could not all be stupid and incompetent. Although he realized he should have seen signs of his partner's shady character, this was after the fact. He still had the skills to run his own company.

This was a major setback, but not a permanent one. Although he had to go back to working for someone else for a couple of years, he continued to look for opportunities to once again start his own business. In a few years, Jim was once again in charge of his own company and, helped by an upturn in the economy, doing very well financially.

Although he was successful in bringing back his business, his marriage was another matter. Things had deteriorated to the point of no return. Jim and Lynn both agreed that it would be better if they divorced. The children were grown up and had left home by that time. Jim recalls that leaving the relationship was the hardest decision he ever had to make in his life. The pain of staying in the relationship was, however, greater than facing all the fears and guilt about leaving.

Drawing on support from his AA group and spiritual beliefs, he went ahead with the divorce. Later, he would realize that he had been lonely for the twenty-one years he had been married. The first and most difficult step in finding the relationship that he wanted involved leaving his marriage. Jim continued to date casually and, through his involvement with an international men's group, met Lisa. As it turned out, Lisa was herself involved in a women's self-development group. Their relationship is still going strong. Both Jim and Lisa strongly believe in facing issues and working through them together. Individually, they are each on a personal journey of growth.

While on his personal quest, Jim spends as much time as possible with his grandchildren and is working hard at maintaining a healthy relationship with his children. Through his efforts, a number of family members, as well as numerous friends and acquaintances, have become involved in his men's organization. Feeling that he has received many gifts in his life, Jim spends countless hours and a great deal of his own money to help others reach their potential. He was recently honored by his community for unselfishly contributing to his community. While up on the podium receiving his award, struggling to hold back emotions, he spoke of his grandfather and the great gift that he had given Jim. Now in his mid-fifties, Jim feels that the most rewarding and challenging parts of his life are still ahead.

"There is only one optimist. He has been here since man has been on this earth, and that is 'man' himself. If we hadn't had such a magnificent optimism to carry us through all these things, we wouldn't be here. We have survived; it is our optimism."

—PHOTOGRAPHER EDWARD STEICHEN

Techniques for Increasing Optimism

o **When difficult situations arise, do what you can to stop them from getting worse immediately.** This will give you a sense of control and momentarily keep you from focusing on the negative.

o **Think of situations that were worse than this that you have overcome in the past.**

o When in a bad situation, think in terms of how it will appear in a month, a year, or ten years from now. How important will it be when you look back on it?

o When stuck focusing upon the negative, find a technique that will help bring you out of it. I have a small, flat, smooth rock that has a great deal of significance to me. I carry it with me and rub it whenever I find myself stuck in fears and negativity. Inevitably, it centers me and allows me to get past the present situation. Find something that has meaning for you.

o Challenge any negative thoughts that you find yourself constantly being drawn into. For example, if you find yourself feeling that nothing ever works out for you, think of all the things that have gone right. Keep a list on a small card in your pocket that you can refer to if the thoughts or feelings are reoccurring.

o Make a habit of celebrating your accomplishments, even small ones. You don't have to celebrate all accomplishments in a big way; just do something that acknowledges the achievement. For example, the other day I was able to help a colleague successfully navigate through a difficult process to register for a course online. I celebrated by treating myself to a huge latte . . . with extra whipped cream on top.

Notes

1. Robin Sharma, *Greatness Guide Book 2* (New York: HarperCollins, 2007), p. 110.
2. Bob Nelson, *1001 Ways to Take Initiative at Work* (New York: Workman Publishing, 1999), p. 37.
3. Robin Sharma, *Greatness Guide Book 2* (New York: HarperCollins, 2007), p. 82.

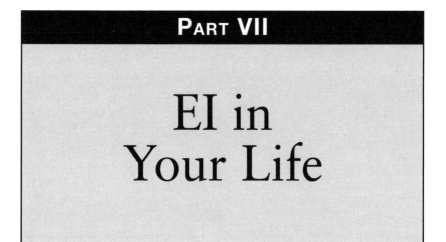

PART **VII**

EI in Your Life

CHAPTER 20

Assessing Your EI

Getting Real About Your Life

"Attack life, it's going to kill you anyway."

—STEVEN COALLIER

T here are situations in our lives in which we come face-to-face with
the reality of our lives. These are instances where we truly see our
lives for what they are, honestly seeing all the joys and sorrows, victo-
ries and failures, celebrations and tragedies. Many years ago as a social
worker freshly graduated from university, I was assigned to work in a
palliative care unit in a hospital. I remember being terrified when I first
was asked to speak to Charles, a man who was dying of cancer. I had no
idea of what I could say to someone who was dying. The patient noticed
my discomfort and said, "Relax Harvey," and then began to talk. At that
moment, I realized that I didn't have to say anything, just listening was
enough. I spent hours listening to Charles and to many other patients
who were spending their last weeks, days, and hours there. Talk about
getting real. These people shared their lives with me, the good times and
bad, their aspirations, joys, and failures. I heard the peace and acceptance
of people who had, on the whole, lived the life that they desired. I also
heard the pain, sorrow, and bitter regrets of those who were unhappy

with many aspects of how their lives turned out.

Whenever I need to get real with myself, I bring my mind back to that time and place. In my imagination, I fast-forward to the end of my life. I see myself in my last days, looking back over my life. No more excuses, justifications, or denials. No more time, no more anything. Nobody to explain to. All of the superficiality totally stripped away. My life reduced down to its most basic essence. I think to myself: Will my life bring me comfort, satisfaction? Did I do the things I really wanted to do? Or was I a martyr, living someone else's life? Did my fears keep me from going after the life I wanted or despite my fears did I go for it?

Whenever I know in my heart that I really want something—and start feeling twinges of fear and doubt—I go to that place, at the end of my life, and imagine what it will feel like if I went for it. There are three different scenarios that play out in my mind.

1. I imagine I went for it and achieved the goal that I was so passionate about. Under this scenario, I imagine feeling peaceful and grateful for a life well lived.
2. I imagine that I tried my best but was unsuccessful. Under this scenario, I feel peaceful, knowing that I gave it my best shot and that it wasn't meant to be. No doubts or questions about what might have been.
3. The last scenario, the one in which I sold myself short by allowing my doubts and fears to overcome me, is a nightmare. I feel regret, sadness, and anger for having let myself down. Far from feeling peaceful and grateful, I am feeling miserable and empty.

So often, the tragedies in our lives are what focus us and cause us to reexamine our lives and make the necessary changes to turn our lives around. Many great works of music, literature, and art have come during or after a very painful period for the creator.

My challenge to you is not to wait for the tragedy to get yourself moving toward the life you want and desire. Do something today, regardless of how small. Do the same thing tomorrow and every day after that.

Giving Up on the Victim

For many years I was a victim. I blamed my lack of success on coming from a disadvantaged background. A number of years ago, I began to realize that whether or not any of this had any merit was totally irrelevant. I began to see that spending energy on things from the past that I could not change was a total waste of time and did not serve me in any way. It only kept me in the victim mode. The only thing I could do to change things was to do everything in my power from that point on to change my life. To this end, I have put up reminders to myself where I can see them daily. This is one way that I remind myself that my future is totally up to me.

> "Nothing in the world can take the place of persistence. Talent will not; nothing is more common than unsuccessful people with talent. Genius will not; unrewarded genius is almost a proverb. Education will not; the world is full of educated derelicts. Persistence and determination alone are omnipotent. The slogan 'press on' has solved and always will solve the problems of the human race."
>
> —FORMER U.S. PRESIDENT CALVIN COOLIDGE

How do you remember to live large? It's not enough to go listen to a motivational speaker once a year. We may feel motivated for a few days but the energy will wear off and we will forget. What we need is a daily habit, a plan to motivate us and keep us moving toward our goals on a daily basis.

Find someone or something that gets you pumped, gets the juices flowing, and makes you feel excited and motivated. Take that person or thing with you on a daily basis in the form of:

- Photos or words on the wall in your office, home, or any other place you spend time in daily

- Recorded music that you listen to in your car, or on your personal music device, that reminds you of that person or thing

- Opening page when you turn on your computer at work and home

- Writings, quotes, or articles by that person posted in a place where you see it every day

> "Life isn't worth living unless you're prepared to take some big chances and go for broke."
>
> —AUTHOR ELIOT WIGGINTON

> "Being on a tightrope is living; everything else is waiting."
>
> —KARL WALLENDA, FOUNDER OF THE FLYING WALLENDAS, AN INTERNATIONAL CIRCUS ACT KNOWN FOR PERFORMING DEATH-DEFYING ACTS WITHOUT A NET

What keeps us from doing what we know we should be doing? We are motivated by how we experience pain and pleasure. Take an experience that is familiar to millions of people all over the globe. Even though we know that we would be better off if we stopped smoking today, we will experience immediate pain in terms of withdrawal and cravings for another cigarette. On the other hand, the prospect of lung cancer and other illnesses, which increase with every cigarette smoked, is down the road at some future distant time. The pleasure we receive from smoking is now, the pain is down the road. The easiest thing to do at the moment, therefore, is to have another cigarette.

Massaging the Pain

One way to quit what we are doing that is hurting us is to increase the pain. A friend of mine who worked in a hospital setting quit smoking temporarily after he saw a patient trying to smoke through a hole in his throat after having a laryngectomy. The fear that he experienced from this sight temporarily made him quit smoking. However, after several months, the memory of the fear wore off and he started smoking again. Had he been able to keep the fear alive for a longer period, he may have been able to quit for good. A work colleague and her daughter, who is a smoker, recently went to see the BodyWorks exhibit of plastinated human bodies. As a result of seeing the blackened lungs of smokers, the daughter quit smoking for a month. What is needed is to find a way to keep the pain in front of a person longer. This is not easy and takes some effort. Perhaps she could have photos of the blackened lungs of lung cancer patients where she could see them daily. Maybe she could have a photo of someone close who died of lung cancer where she could see it daily. Recently, a woman who was diagnosed with terminal lung cancer went around to schools talking about the dangers of smoking. She continued right until the time she was admitted to the hospital. The sight of her, with her bald head from chemotherapy treatments and emaciated appearance, was meant to show the pain of smoking to students who were smoking or might be tempted to start.

Becoming Your Own Best Friend

If you were to die tomorrow, what would people say about you at your funeral? How many people would be there? What sort of memories of you would they have? What would you like to have written on your tombstone? Is it true of the person you are today?

Do You Like Yourself?

Ask yourself the following questions:

- When I think of buying myself something expensive, do I ever have thoughts that I am not worth it?

- Do I feel myself shrinking into the background when a powerful person is around?

- When asked to do something new at work or given more responsibility, do I have doubts as to my abilities?

- Am I attractive, average, or below average in appearance? What makes me think that I am? How do I feel when in the presence of someone I consider to be more attractive than me? Someone who is much more attractive?

o Am I smart and talented? How do I feel around people who I see as smarter and more talented?

o What about my friends? Are they attractive? Talented? Successful? Do I look at people and tell myself that I could never be friends with them because they are too good looking or smart? The people you choose to associate with and how you view them will tell you a great deal about how you view yourself.

When you answer these questions honestly, you will get a good picture of how you feel about yourself. If you feel overall positive and upbeat after pondering these questions, you likely have a healthy relationship with yourself. If you are having lingering discomforting thoughts, it is an indication that there are things about you that need changing.

Getting Real About Your Relationships

In order for us to gain control over our own destiny, we must ask ourselves some basic questions and honestly look for the answers. The first question that we must ask is: Is my life working for me? This requires asking ourselves some tough questions.

Relationships with Others

Do I have the types of relationships that I really want? Are my relationships with my partner and children healthy ones? Am I settling for less because of fear, or thoughts that this is as good as it gets? Or perhaps I think I don't deserve any better. What about friends? Do I have the type of friends I'm proud of and am always happy to spend time with? Are they supportive of me and I of them? Or are they people I settle for, maybe even feel resentment or jealousy toward?

We have all felt in our relationships from time to time some resentment or jealousy toward the other person. However, be honest about what your predominant thoughts are toward that person. If you aren't sure or are so engrossed that you have a hard time sorting them out, sit down with a piece of paper. On one side put down all the positive things you normally think of this person. On the other side, write down your negative thoughts. What do you come up with?

Ask yourself the following questions:

- If I had to do it over again, would I choose the same partner or friends?

- If I could have any partner or friends that I wanted, would I choose the ones I have today?

- How do I feel (honestly) when I introduce my partner or friends to others? Do I feel proud, grateful to have them as part of my life? Do I feel that I have to explain something about them to others? Do I sometimes feel ashamed or embarrassed?

- How do I feel when I'm with that person? Do I feel secure, loved, cared about, and appreciated? Or am I on edge, anxious or fearful about what they might say or do?

- Do I often make excuses for the partner that I have or my friends? Do I find myself defending their behavior to others a lot?

- Do my partner and friends have healthy and supportive networks of their own or do their networks appear limited?

- Do I like and get along with most of my partner's family and friends? How about friends? Do I get along with and like the friends of my friends?

- When my partner receives major recognition for an achievement, money, or some other reward, am I genuinely happy for him or her, or do I (openly or secretly) resent my partner's success? How about with my friends?

When you ask yourself these questions, what do you come up with? If you are able to answer yes to most or many of these questions, you are likely doing many things right in your relationships. You have been able to develop and sustain healthy relationships in all aspects of your life. If not, when will the pain of staying in these relationships become great enough that you will begin doing the difficult work necessary to break free?

If you find that no has been the predominant answer to most of these questions, you have some work to do in the relationship aspects of your life. Determine what the cause is, and look for a common denominator. Is it you? Answer this question honestly. Which of these relationships is worth saving and which, in your heart, do you wish you did not have in your life. You don't have to make these changes overnight but come up with a game plan. Use Chapter 11: Healthy Relationships to come up with some ideas for making changes.

CHAPTER 21

Increasing Your EI

Where Do I Begin?

"Life is either a daring adventure, or nothing."

—Helen Keller, American Author
Who was Blind, Deaf, and Mute

S tart with where you are. As you were reading through the book, you were likely having a conversation with yourself. In certain chapters, you may have been telling yourself, "This is something that I'm really good at." In others, you may have said, "Here's something that I really have a problem with." Other chapters may have brought out a more neutral response and you found yourself saying, "I'm not too bad at this. Not great, but not too bad." Trust your instincts on your self-judgments. If you want a second opinion, ask someone close to you whom you trust and know will tell you the truth. You can always take the BarOn EQ-i assessment. However, please don't feel that you need to do this assessment. In most cases, the people to whom I have administered the BarOn EQ-i have accurately predicted both their highest and lowest scores on the test. I'm betting that if you have read the book up to this point and have an interest in EI, you already have a good dose of self-awareness. In that case, I'm betting that you already have a good sense of where you would score in all the areas and the BarOn EQ-i would only confirm what you already know.

The question then becomes: What if I find myself needing help in a number of areas? Where do I start? What area do I work on first or do I work on all of them at the same time? Are some areas more important than others? Are some areas prerequisites of becoming successful in others?

Where Do I Start?

Start from the inside out. The inner world is the base for growth in all areas of your life. Your success in all the other areas and the amount of progress that you make will depend on how well you understand yourself and how well you think of yourself. A good sense of self-awareness and healthy self-regard are crucial. If you were a tree, your self-regard would be the roots. It is what sustains and nurtures you and on which everything else depends. You've likely heard the saying that no one can feel good about you unless you feel good about yourself. How true. Don't confuse healthy self-regard with conceit and arrogance. Many of us were brought up with the idea that humility was a virtue and may associate feeling good about ourselves with arrogance. But arrogance is the result of the ego being out of control, and is not about self-regard. It is all right to feel good about you—in fact, it is a prerequisite to all the good things in life.

> "You are a child of God. Your playing small does not serve the world. There is nothing enlightened about shrinking so that other people won't feel insecure about you. We are born to manifest the glory of God that is within us."
>
> —NELSON ROCKEFELLER, FORMER U.S. VICE PRESIDENT, PHILANTHROPIST, AND BUSINESSMAN

If you are struggling in the areas of self-awareness and self-regard, focus on those and don't worry about the rest for now. Once you feel good about yourself, you will be better equipped to work on other areas.

○ **What if my inner world is okay, but I have some other areas that could use some improvement?** The type of personal change we are talking about occurs because of consistent focus and effort over a period of time. For me, it works better to focus on one area and work on it consistently over a period of time. Consistency and time are important elements for transformational change. The important thing is that you stick with whatever you choose to take on for a long enough period of time so that you and others will notice a change. Often people, in a moment of enthusiasm and energy, want to change their lives overnight. After a short period of time, they are feeling overwhelmed, and not seeing any evidence of change, so they give up on the entire program. Don't set yourself up for failure by getting caught up in wanting to change overnight.

○ **If my inner world is in good shape, but I need work in a number of other areas, how do I prioritize them?** Whatever you are drawn to most is the area that I would focus on first. There is one exception and that is impulse control. A person with poor impulse control is like a walking powder keg looking for a flame. If that is an area of work for you, I would focus on it before the other areas. The reason is that poor impulse control can cause serious problems regardless of other areas you might be strong in. Saying the wrong thing at the wrong time has caused serious and irreversible damage to careers, marriages, and relationships. Once it is said, you can never take it back. Think of slips of the tongue that have ended otherwise successful political, acting, and other high-profile careers. If this is a problem area, act now to get it under your control. The other areas can wait until you feel you have this aspect under control.

○ **Where do I focus my efforts, on my workplace or on my home?** The benefits of increasing your emotional intelligence will be felt in both your home and workplace. If you are able to communicate better with your spouse and develop a more rewarding relationship, you will be happier at work. The skills from building the relationship at home can be transferred to the workplace. Pick the area of your world that is the most urgent, the most volatile. Focus on the area that is causing you the most distress in your life at this time.

○ **What about my high scores? Do I just ignore them and work on the areas that I am weaker in?** That's a great question and one that is not often considered in the EI world. Typically, the first thing that people notice when receiving the results of any test is their low scores. That's unfortunate as there is a growing movement in psychology (especially in positive psychology) that tells us that we are better off if we focus on our strengths instead. The usual approach is for us to concentrate on our areas of improvement and spend little time on our strengths.

Contrarian author Marcus Buckingham in *Go Put Your Strengths to Work* believes that in our workplaces we should not spend so much time and effort looking at our weaknesses, rather we should focus on and improve our strengths. Buckingham advances the theory that since our strengths are what we love to do, we will gain much more by working on our strengths and looking for situations to make use of them. On the other hand, he claims that we will have a more difficult time making progress working on our areas of weakness because we will lack motivation to change them and it will always feel like a great struggle to attempt to do so.

For example, my strongest EI area is independence. It explains why I have struggled in bureaucratic types of positions in which there are layers of decision-making authority and little room for innovation and creativity. In order for me to be most effective, productive, and happy in life, I need to work in an area where I have a great deal of independence, the ability to be innovative, and try out new ideas that come to me.

Being aware of our strengths helps us to make better decisions when it comes to career directions and personal relationships. We will naturally gravitate to the areas that use our greatest strengths. With the exercises in this book, we can increase our higher scores as well and reach an even higher level in an area that we are already strong in. If we are fortunate enough to have strengths in all of the areas, we can choose which areas we want to take to the next level. Life will become a joy and an ongoing adventure.

When we are strong in all areas of emotional intelligence, life will seem like a daring adventure, one in which we can fully participate. The exciting thing is that we can all increase our EI to that point if we make up our minds to do so.

How We Think Is Crucial to Our Success

One of the things that I do is print off my strengths on my computer and hang them on the wall where I can see them. They say something like this: I AM ALREADY VERY INDEPENDENT AND A GREAT PROBLEM SOLVER. On another piece of paper I write: SOON I WILL HAVE GREATER IMPULSE CONTROL AND BECOME MORE FLEXIBLE. These signs remind me of my strengths and the areas that I am working on. Notice that I didn't put down that I was weak at impulse control and flexibility. That would be a negative statement. I turned it into a positive by stating that I was getting better in these areas. How we think about ourselves is crucial to how successful we will be. There is incredible power in being able to imagine or envision ourselves obtaining something, gaining a skill, or becoming a certain type of person.

> "Whether you think you can, or you think you can't, either way you'll be right."
>
> —HENRY FORD,
> AMERICAN INDUSTRIALIST AND AUTOMOTIVE PIONEER

When we look at areas in our lives that need improvement, it is extremely important that we look at these areas only as temporary indicators of where we are in the present. The next step is to imagine ourselves drastically improving in those areas. Imagine the good things that will come to us when we become happier, more optimistic, and improve in whatever area we are working on. Finally, we need to come up with basic improvement exercises and a plan to put these into action and keep doing them for an extended period of time. Over time, these exercises may become so integrated and even enjoyable that they become a part of us. Allen's story is a good example.

Allen's Story

Allen grew up a shy, introverted kid without a lot of friends. In high school, he wasn't one of the popular kids but hung around with a couple of classmates who were as shy as he was. Nobody in his group dated, envying the popular guys who seemed to be able to talk to and joke around with the girls effortlessly. He wasn't bad looking and there were girls who were interested in him, but they soon gave up as Allen's shyness made him seem disinterested.

Once people got to know Allen, they realized that he had a great sense of humor, was bright, articulate, and sensitive. The trouble was that it was difficult to get to know him and most people didn't put forth the effort. It was only well into his adulthood that Allen decided that he needed to do something to turn his life around. At work, even though Allen did a great job, he was often overlooked because he did not speak up at meetings and was overshadowed by those who were more outgoing. As a result, others who were less talented and didn't work as hard as he did were promoted over him. Allen always admired people who could start conversations with complete strangers. He decided that he would start to do this. At first it felt very awkward, even painful, but he set a goal of striking up a certain number of conversations with strangers. Five years later, Allen is a changed person. He still strikes up conversations with strangers, but now he does it not out of a challenge or for self-improvement, he actually enjoys doing it. Now more confident and outgoing, Allen finds himself speaking up more in all areas including work and social occasions. At work, he has been recently promoted as he now seldom leaves a meeting without getting in what he wants to say. In the past, he dreaded parties and ended up sitting in a corner or hanging out at the edges of groups listening in to their conversations. Allen now looks forward to parties and has met and dated a fair share of women whom he has met there. Allen's advice for those who are shy is to "just get out there and do it! It's hard at first, but it gets easier over time and you start to really enjoy your life. Life is much too short and precious to sit around on the outside looking in."

Allen was motivated to change his life and envisioned what it could be like. Those two crucial factors led to the success that he now thoroughly enjoys.

The Power of Gratitude

Virtually every book on personal change and growth that I have read speaks about the importance of gratitude. I believe that cultivating a gratitude habit is essential to any kind of success in life. Whenever I find myself dwelling on negative thoughts, facing doubts, and not experiencing good feelings, I know that the quickest and easiest way to break free of those thoughts is to go to a place of gratitude. As soon as I start to look for, and focus on, the things that I am grateful for, my whole perspective on the world changes. I start feeling good inside and as a result my thoughts become more positive. I focus on what I want instead of what I don't want.

Gratitude is a good base from which to build all of the EI areas. Most highly successful people, when interviewed about their success, talk about gratitude as something that they practice on a daily basis. When we are feeling grateful, we naturally drift toward feeling happier and more optimistic. When we are feeling stressed, reminding ourselves of all the good things in our lives can take off some of the pressure. My friend Sheldon was going through a very steep learning curve in a new job several years ago. Many days he felt like he was working in a pressure cooker, expected to learn a great deal in a very short time. Sheldon was separated from his partner and had joint custody of their eight-year-old daughter, Lisee. Whenever the pressure at work started to get to Sheldon, he would focus on how grateful he was to have Lisee. At that point, he realized that even if the worst-case scenario of losing his job happened, the things that really mattered, such as Lisee, would still be there. Whenever he thought of Lisee, he immediately felt released from a great deal of tension. This allowed him to get through this difficult early period of the job. He has gone on to make a long and successful career with this organization.

Purpose

The aim of EI is to address the "how" of life. It addresses the question of how to become more successful at work and home so that we can live more fulfilling and rewarding lives. It does not address the more fundamental question of why. Before we can talk about how we can live better lives, we need to have a compelling reason to do so. We need to have a purpose. Answering the question of our purpose here on earth has been the basis of much debate among philosophers, religious groups, and thinkers since the beginning of time.

According to some philosophies, having a purpose is the core of all good in human life. Man's search for meaning, according to well-known psychiatrist, author, and concentration camp survivor Victor Frankl, is the primary motivating force in life. Helen Keller felt that happiness comes from "fidelity to a worthy purpose." The Dalai Lama connects purpose and happiness in that he feels that the purpose of life is the pursuit of happiness. This takes a more direct approach to purpose than other philosophies that espouse that our purpose is to help others and make the planet a better place to live, which will lead to happiness. Whichever comes first may be a question that writers and thinkers will debate forever. The point, however, is that there is a strong connection between altruism and happiness.

There are two basic beliefs regarding whether we choose our own purpose or whether it is chosen by a power greater than us. On the one hand, we have the belief that there is an inherent purpose in life that has been chosen by God. On the other hand, there are scientific points of view that state that there is no inherent purpose in life and it is up to the individual to find his or her own purpose.

It is beyond the scope of this book to help you find your purpose or to get into the purpose debate in any way. It is important to find your purpose in life because it forms the foundation for everything that you think, feel, and do. It is my belief that the tools and techniques in this book will help you reach your potential and fulfill your purpose, whatever it may be.

Questions and Answers

Q: What is emotional intelligence?

A: Emotional intelligence refers to an array of attributes and tools that enable us to deal with the pressures and demands of our environment. EI has been referred to as common sense or advanced common sense. Street smarts is another term that has been used in conjunction with EI.

Q: Why should I learn more about emotional intelligence?

A: The short, simple answer is to be more successful and fulfilled in your life. A great deal of testing in the workplace has shown that from 27 to 45 percent of success on the job is determined by our EI. Other results have shown that people who scored higher on EI tests reported higher satisfaction in their relationships with their partners. Since we use our emotions in all areas of our lives, it makes sense that increasing our capabilities in one area will positively impact all the others.

Q: How do I find out how much emotional intelligence I have?

A: The obvious and best way is to take the BarOn EQ-i assessment.

However, if you don't wish to go this route, there are other ways. My experience with administering this instrument tells me that most people with a good sense of self-awareness have a fairly good idea of where their strengths and weaknesses are. Be aware of your reactions to the different chapters in the book. This will give you a good indication of your strengths and areas for growth. Ask an aware person who knows you well and will be honest in giving you feedback.

Q: What if I find out that I have low emotional intelligence; won't that be difficult to accept?

A: This fear is a common one and understandable. It is natural to want to score high in all areas. It is important if experiencing this fear to remember a few important things:

1. The great thing about EI, unlike IQ, is that we can increase our scores. The score on the assessment is only the starting point.

2. In this case, not knowing can hurt you and likely has prevented you from furthering your potential. Awareness is the first step toward change and improvement.

Q: How long will it take me to increase my EI?

A: This is a very difficult question to answer. It all depends on where you are now and how much time, effort, and perseverance you put into your improvement plan. Some theorists claim that it takes at least a year of continuous repetitive effort to change a behavior. Again, it depends on the individual and situation.

Q: What do I need to do to increase my EI?

A: You cannot increase your EI through reading about it. The reading is only for gathering information and increasing knowledge. To improve your EI, you need to practice new approaches with others consistently over a long period of time. There are techniques at the end of every chapter for increasing the particular attribute talked about in the chapter.

Improvements in many areas of EI will raise other areas, as many of the attributes are interconnected. For example, if your self-regard increases, other areas such as independence and stress tolerance will likely go up as well. Likewise, seeing positive changes in any of the areas is likely to give your self-regard a boost.

Q: What is the relationship between IQ and EI?

A: Research shows no correlation between the two. In other words, one cannot predict the other. Your chance of having high EI along with high IQ is just as great as your chance of having low EI with high IQ.

Of the research that has been done in the workplace, the average correlation between IQ and success is around 6 percent. The correlation between EI and success in the workplace is between 27 and 45 percent, depending on the industry. In other words, EI is a much greater predictor of success than IQ.

Q: Is EI inherited or is it learned?

A: There is no doubt that we are each born with different innate qualities. In addition, our environment—such as the modeling and teaching of our parents and encouragement we received growing up—contributes to our EI. However, we do know that everyone can improve their EI through effort, so that regardless of what you were born with you can increase it if you desire.

Q: Does this mean if my EI is at a higher level, I don't need to have a high IQ?

A: There are many people who are very successful who would not score extremely high on an IQ test. The ideal, of course, would be to have both a high IQ and EI. Having a high EI will allow you to take advantage of a high IQ. In many cases, having poor EI will result in any advantage from a high IQ being squandered. I'm sure you know of some genius who is not getting the most out of life due to lacking in some form of people skills.

Mini EI Quiz

This short assessment will give you an idea of what emotional intelligence is about. It is not meant to be a serious test of your emotional functioning, so have fun with it.

For a comprehensive test of emotional intelligence that has been scientifically validated, I recommend the BarOn EQ-i, which is the assessment this book is based on.

If you are going through some trauma in your life, the results may be quite skewed and not a good indication of where you truly are. Wait until things return to a more normal state before doing the quiz.

Note: When answering the questions, please stay focused on what the question asks. Because of the way the questions are set up, it is easy to answer the opposite way from what you intended.

1. When I have a strong emotional reaction, I am usually able to relate it to an experience from my past.
   1. Not true of me
   2. Seldom true of me
   3. Sometimes true of me
   4. Often true of me
   5. True of me

2. I have no difficulty asking for what I want.
   1. Not true of me
   2. Seldom true of me
   3. Sometimes true of me
   4. Often true of me
   5. True of me

3. The people whom I choose to spend time with are supportive of me and my goals.
   1. Not true of me
   2. Seldom true of me
   3. Sometimes true of me
   4. Often true of me
   5. True of me

4. I am satisfied with what I have achieved in life.
   1. Not true of me
   2. Seldom true of me
   3. Sometimes true of me
   4. Often true of me
   5. True of me

5. I rely on my own judgment in making decisions.
   1. Not true of me
   2. Seldom true of me
   3. Sometimes true of me
   4. Often true of me
   5. True of me

6. I am able to understand why others feel the way they do.
   1. Not true of me
   2. Seldom true of me
   3. Sometimes true of me
   4. Often true of me
   5. True of me

7. In conversations, I often ask others about themselves and their world.
   1. Not true of me
   2. Seldom true of me
   3. Sometimes true of me
   4. Often true of me
   5. True of me

8. I believe that helping others is an important part of life.
   1. Not true of me
   2. Seldom true of me
   3. Sometimes true of me
   4. Often true of me
   5. True of me

9. Solving problems comes easily to me.
   1. Not true of me
   2. Seldom true of me
   3. Sometimes true of me
   4. Often true of me
   5. True of me

10. Understanding the way others see things is easy for me.
    1. Not true of me
    2. Seldom true of me
    3. Sometimes true of me
    4. Often true of me
    5. True of me

11. I adapt easily to change.
    1. Not true of me
    2. Seldom true of me
    3. Sometimes true of me
    4. Often true of me
    5. True of me

12. I seldom let pressure get to me.
    1. Not true of me
    2. Seldom true of me
    3. Sometimes true of me
    4. Often true of me
    5. True of me

13. I rarely speak or act without thinking things through.
    1. Not true of me
    2. Seldom true of me
    3. Sometimes true of me
    4. Often true of me
    5. True of me

14. Most of the time it feels great to be alive.
    1. Not true of me
    2. Seldom true of me
    3. Sometimes true of me
    4. Often true of me
    5. True of me

15. I expect things to get better in the future.
    1. Not true of me
    2. Seldom true of me
    3. Sometimes true of me
    4. Often true of me
    5. True of me

Add up your numbers from all of your answers. The results are below.

Results of Harvey's EI Quiz:

60–75 Congratulations! Indications are that you are doing very well in the high end of the emotional intelligence scale. You know yourself well and have developed healthy, sustaining relationships with others. You are usually happy and optimistic, and feel quite good about what you have accomplished in your life. Because you already have a solid base, your potential to develop to an even higher level by using EI is excellent.

45–59 Your score indicates that you are doing fairly well. Your self-awareness and relationships with others are above average. You have achievements you are proud of, are generally in a good mood, and see the world in a positive way. There is still room for improvement in all areas and there are times when you feel you are capable of doing/achieving more than you have. By diligently using EI tools, you are able to get even more from life.

30–44 Your score indicates that you are struggling somewhat with how you feel about yourself and your relationships with others. You are aware of this and are likely open to making some changes. The good news is that you can make significant changes by diligently practicing new positive EI behaviors.

15–29 Give yourself credit for answering honestly. Your results indicate that your life is a difficult struggle in a number of areas. The good news is that you are able to make significant changes to your life if you are willing to do what is required. There are countless stories of people who have made drastic changes despite coming from a difficult place. You will find that once you start seeing changes resulting from your efforts you will begin feeling much more positive about your life.

For further information on the BarOn EQ-i assessment, contact:

Multi Health Systems
emotionalintelligence@mhs.com
1-800-456-3003 in the United States
1-800-268-6001 in Canada

Recommended Reading

Baker, Dan, Ph.D., and Cameron Stauth. *What Happy People Know: How the New Science of Happiness Can Change Your Life for the Better.* New York: St. Martin's Griffin, 2003.
*Ways to increase happiness

Buckingham, Marcus. *Go Put Your Strengths to Work: Six Powerful Steps to Achieve Maximum Performance.* New York: Simon & Schuster, 2007.

Byrne, Rhonda. *The Secret.* New York: Atria Books, 2006.

Covey, Stephen R. *The 7 Habits of Highly Effective People: Powerful Lessons in Personal Change.* New York: Fireside Books, 1990.

Csikszentmihalyi, Mihaly. *Flow: The Psychology of Optimal Experience.* New York: Harper & Row Publishers, 1990.
*Interesting information about happiness and self-actualization

Freedman, Joshua. *At the Heart of Leadership: How to Get Results with Emotional Intelligence.* San Mateo, CA: Six Seconds, 2007.

Goleman, Daniel. *Emotional Intelligence: Why It Can Matter More Than IQ.* New York: Bantam House New York, 1995.

————. *Working with Emotional Intelligence*. New York: Bantam House, 1998.

————. Richard Boyatzis, and Annie McKee. *Primal Leadership: Realizing the Power of Emotional Intelligence*. Boston: Harvard Business School Publishing, 2002.

Gray, John. *Men Are from Mars, Women Are from Venus: A Classic Guide to Understanding the Opposite Sex*. New York: Harper Paperback, 2004.
*Good tips for building EI in relationships with the opposite sex

Grubbs-West, Lorraine. *Lessons in Loyalty: How Southwest Airlines Does It–An Insider's View*. Dallas: CornerStone Leadership Institute, 2005.
*Ideas for building an EI workplace

Kerr, Michael. *Inspiring Workplaces: Creating the Kind of Workplace Where Everyone Wants to Work*. Canada: Humor at Work Institute.
*Ideas for putting EI into the workplace

Litwin, Val, Brad Stokes, Erik Hanson, and Chris Bratseth. *Cool to Be Kind: Random Acts and How to Commit Them*. Toronto: ECW Press, 2004.
*Focuses on social responsibility

Lynn, Adele B. *The EQ Interview: Finding Employees with High Emotional Intelligence*. New York: AMACOM, 2008.
*An excellent EI guide for human resource professionals

Maxwell, John C. *Relationships 101: What Every Leader Needs to Know*. Nashville: Thomas Nelson, 2004.

McGraw, Phillip C., Ph.D. *Self Matters: Creating Your Life from the Inside Out*. New York: Simon & Schuster, 2001.
*Good primer for boosting self-regard

Robbins, Anthony. *Awaken the Giant Within: How to Take Immediate Control of Your Mental, Emotional, Physical, and Financial Destiny*. New York: Simon & Schuster, 1991.

Seligman, Martin, Ph.D. *Learned Optimism: How to Change Your Mind and Your Life*. New York: Free Press, 1998.
*Ways of increasing optimism

Sharma, Robin. *Greatness Guide Book 2: 101 More Insights to Get You to World Class*. Toronto: HarperCollins, 2007.

Shimoff, Marci, with Carol Kline. *Happy for No Reason: 7 Steps to Being Happy from the Inside Out*. New York: Free Press, 2008.
*Ideas to increase happiness

Stein, Steven J., Ph.D., and Howard E. Book, M.D. *The EQ Edge: Emotional Intelligence and Your Success*. Toronto, Canada: John Wiley & Sons, 1996.
*Great stories and tips on increasing all aspects of EI in all areas of our lives

Sternberg, Robert J. *Successful Intelligence: How Practical and Creative Intelligence Determine Success in Life*. New York: Plume Books, 1997.

Tracy, Brian. *Maximum Achievement: Strategies and Skills That Will Unlock Your Hidden Powers to Succeed*. New York: Simon & Schuster, 1995.

Williamson, Marianne. *Everyday Grace*. New York: Riverhead Trade, 2004.

Websites

www.EQ.org—directory of hundreds of EQ websites and services.

www.6seconds.org—Six Seconds, the Emotional Intelligence Network, provides information and innovative tools to help change agents make a positive difference.

www.Eiconsortium.org—research on application of EQ in organizations.

www.sixseconds.com—Six Seconds Consulting partners with leaders to create a climate where teams excel and talent thrives.

www.NexusEQ.com—premier international EQ conference.

www.mhs.com—providing psychological assessments for more than twenty years, including the BarOn Emotional Quotient Inventory (EQ-i) and the Mayer-Salovey-Caruso Emotional Intelligence Test (MSCEIT).

www.peoplesmithglobal.com—coaching and training for individuals and organizations using EQ.

www.davidcory.com—an emotional intelligence training company. David Cory is a certified trainer in the area of emotional intelligence with MHS Inc. and is considered to be an international expert on the integration of emotional intelligence and leadership development.

www.leabrovedani.com—speaker and emotional intelligence expert, Lea's forte is team building in organizations.

www.talentsmart.com—books, selection tool, and leading emotional intelligent assessments to develop an emotionally intelligent workforce.

www.haygroup.com/TL—provides tools, measures, and data to help people and organizations change.

Organizations for Boosting EI

Toastmasters

As a member of this great organization, I can't say enough good things about it. Presentation skills have been shown to be crucial to how successful we are in the workplace. Toastmasters helps you develop your public speaking and leadership skills. While increasing your ability and confidence in public speaking in a supportive environment, there are many other worthwhile side benefits to belonging to this organization, including:

- Increase self-regard in all areas
- Develop team-building skills
- Increase sense of community and belonging
- Increase flexibility through exposure to diverse ideas and members
- Reduce the stress of public speaking and presentations

Volunteer Service Organizations

There are far too many of these organizations to name here but I believe that volunteering your time to an organization whose goal is to help the less fortunate is an excellent way to increase your sense of social responsibility and become happier and more optimistic. Three of the organizations that I have had experience with and strongly believe in are Big Brothers, Big Sisters, and the Boys and Girls Clubs.

Index

Coolidge, Calvin, on persistence, 183
Cooper, Albert, 147
Covey, Stephen, 88
Csikszentmihalyi, Mihaly, 58–59, 162–163
customer service, 91–92

Dalai Lama, 196
Davis, Bette, on being sure of herself, 54
delayed gratification, 147–148
see also impulse control
DeVos, Richard M., on a positive push, 173
Dick, Philip K., on reality, 121
Doll, Edgar, 15
Donne, John, on interdependence, 97
Dylan, Bob, on success, 63

Edison, Thomas, 67
EI, *see* emotional intelligence
Einstein, Albert, on reality, 118
Eliot, Robert S., on small stuff, 139
Ellis, Albert, 9–10
Emerson, Ralph Waldo
on leadership, 18
on making yourself necessary, 92
Emmons, Robert, 100–101
emotional bank account, 88–89
Emotional Intelligence (Daniel Goleman), 10–11
emotional intelligence (EI), 9–13
correlation of IQ and, 199
definition of, 197
gender differences in, 12–13
history of, 9–11
mini quiz on, 200–204
misconceptions about, 11–12
school programs for developing, 31–32
and success in life, 32, 199
see also assessing emotional intelligence; increasing emotional intelligence
Emotional Intelligence in the Workplace (Daniel Goleman), 11
emotional quotient (EQ), 10
emotional self-awareness, 35–41
example of, 38–40
in increasing EI, 190

and source of emotions, 37
techniques for increasing, 36–37, 40–41
emotions
acknowledging, 81–82
identifying sources of, 37
immediately dealing with, 151
in work environment, 15–16, 25–26, 28
empathy, 75–86
definition of, 75
examples of, 78–80, 82–85
and power of acknowledging feelings, 81–82
and social responsibility, 100
and success in sales, 77
sympathy vs., 75–77
techniques for increasing, 86
end-of-life exercises, 182, 185
The EQ Edge (Steven J. Stein and Howard E. Book), 76–77
EQ (emotional quotient), 10
Evans, Audrey, 101

failure, 169–170
feedback, on strengths, 3
Feynman, Richard, on fooling yourself, 35
flexibility, 125–135
and age, 130
and attitude toward change, 128–129
enhancing, 129–130
example of, 131–133
and mistakes, 130–131
and optimism, 171
qualities related to, 127–128
and success, 126–127
techniques for increasing, 134–135
flow, 58–59
Flow (Mihaly Csikszentmihalyi), 58–59, 162–163
focus, 162–163
Ford, Henry, on thinking, 193
Frankl, Victor, 163, 196
Friedman, Stewart D., 30

Gandhi, Mohandas, on becoming change, 38, 131

INDEX

INDEX